Praise for

Loud and Clear

ALSO BY ANNA QUINDLEN

Blessings
A Short Guide to a Happy Life
How Reading Changed My Life
Black and Blue
One True Thing
Object Lessons
Living Out Loud
Thinking Out Loud
Being Perfect

BOOKS FOR CHILDREN

The Tree That Came to Stay
Happily Ever After

Loud and Clear

Loud
and
Clear

Anna
Quindlen

BALLANTINE BOOKS · NEW YORK

2005 Ballantine Books Trade Paperback Edition

Copyright © 2004 by Anna Quindlen

Published in the United States by Ballantine Books, an imprint of
The Random House Publishing Group, a division of Random House,
Inc., New York.

BALLANTINE and colophon are registered trademarks of Random
House, Inc.

Originally published in hardcover in slightly different form by
Random House, an imprint of The Random House Publishing
Group, a division of Random House, Inc., in 2004.

All the essays that appear in this work were originally published in
Newsweek.

LIBRARY OF CONGRESS CATALOGING-IN-PUBLICATION DATA
Quindlen, Anna.
Loud and clear / Anna Quindlen.
p.   cm.
ISBN 0-8129-7027-6
I. Title.
PS3567.U336L68 2004
814'.54—dc22   2003058625

Printed in the United States of America

Ballantine Books website address: www.ballantinebooks.com

9 8 7 6 5 4 3 2 1

For Houj

I believe that unarmed truth

and unconditional love

will have the final word.

MARTIN LUTHER KING, JR.

Contents

2 MIND

3 BODY

Loud and Clear

Preface

ON THE MORNING OF SEPTEMBER 11, 2001, I was doing what I do as well as anyone I know: that is, not writing. This is an enduring part of my daily routine, something like the unbirthday party in *Through the Looking-Glass*. Unlike some of my colleagues—mainly the ones I don't really care for—I do not fly to my desk each morning with a full heart and a ready hand. I skirt the perimeters of my home office with a sense of dread, eyes averted from an empty computer screen. Instead of creation there is always procrastination: the call to my closest friend to chew over the morning paper and to gossip, which sometimes comes to the same thing; the power walk in Central Park and the interlude at Starbucks—my husband calls it Four-bucks—and the triple venti no-foam latte. Luckily the laundry room is five stories below my office, or I could surely eke out another half hour folding sheets and T-shirts. Several years ago my daughter downloaded a computer game called Snood onto my laptop and for months, before I had used up all the demonstration games, I played over and over in single-minded pursuit of nothing more than a position on a scoreboard that only I ever saw and on which I was known as Big Mama. Eventually I deleted the program. I had developed a terrible Tetris problem a decade earlier that had enabled me to put off writing until well past 10:00 A.M., and I could see which way things were headed.

I am a creature of habit; it is all that allows me to write in the first place, the routine designed to ward off the moment, and then the moment itself, when the first feeble sentence, often merely a prelude to better things, appears as my fingers play word jazz on the keyboard. What follows is usually a manic two or three hours fed by caffeine and the CD of the moment. Sondheim, Tori Amos, Rosemary Clooney, James Taylor, Alanis Morissette. I did not want to learn to type, but the nuns insisted, saying someday I might marry a man who would need his papers typed or be employed by a man who needed the same done to his business letters. My fingers are the only sure-handed things about me when I first sit down to write. After all those years in newsrooms I am a very fast typist indeed, as fast as any executive secretary.

But it was the variation from routine that enables me to remember that morning in particular, remember it before it became the morning of the most important day in the history of the United States during my lifetime. It was my eldest child's eighteenth birthday, and that morning at breakfast his father and I had recalled with clarity and more than a little schmaltz the stiflingly hot morning when he had arrived, limp and gray after a forceps delivery. Twelve days before we had left him at college for the first time, and we were still smarting from the fissure in our family. Before we got into the car and drove away, we reminded him yet again that when he turned eighteen he was obliged by law to go to the post office and register with the Selective Service. Neither of us felt any fear when we told him to do that; it seemed almost quaint, that particular demand at that moment in time from the two of us, the former boy who had lived through the Vietnam draft lottery, the former girlfriend who had stood by breathless waiting for his number to come up, the young couple exhaling in relief after. If I had thought there was any chance my son would be forced to go to war, I would have bought him a ticket to Canada instead of driving him to Connecticut.

There were two other reasons that I remember that morning so clearly as well. The day before my daughter and I had attended the funeral of a family friend in Pennsylvania, and once I was done with my nonwriting rituals I intended to write about her, about the considerable inspiration that the lives of valiant older people provide us. I had gone straight from that funeral to a hospital, where my closest friend was having cancer surgery, surgery that appeared to have been spectacularly successful. So while I have a great deal of trouble remembering almost anything at this moment in my life—while I once did a column tied to my age called "Life in the 30s," I now say that the fifties version would be entitled "Where the Hell Did I Leave My Keys?"—I do remember how I felt that particular morning as I settled into the old Windsor chair at which I finally, finished with preliminaries, sat down to write. I felt painfully mortal, quite vulnerable, and enormously grateful.

Over the course of the next few days the entire city in which I work, the entire country in which I live, would come to feel much the same way.

For me there was a peculiar reason for gratitude as the horrible events of that day unspooled in a long endless loop of cataclysmic news footage. When my husband called to tell me to turn on the television, we both thought there had been a freak accident. But as I watched the arc of that second plane as it smashed into the Trade Center towers just a few miles south of our narrow

Victorian row house, I knew that something uniquely terrible was taking place. I also had reason to believe that everyone I cared for most was safe: My husband across the Hudson at his office. The children at their schools. My friend in the hospital across town. It was difficult for us to talk to one another, of course, with the New York City telephone lines out, the tunnels and bridges shut down, and cyberspace hopelessly jammed. One of the mementos I have kept from that morning are three identical e-mails from our son at college, who could not get through on the day of his birthday or for three days afterward. Each one is dated September 11, 2001, and says in capital letters I REALLY NEED TO HEAR YOUR VOICE.

The morning after, a new world burned and bloomed, too, beneath an incongruously cerulean sky. A group of my daughter's friends gathered in our kitchen and made hundreds of sandwiches and brownies to take to the Red Cross offices nearby. They bought enormous bags of dog food to bring to the local firehouse for their dalmatians and the rescue dogs looking for survivors downtown. The familiar strangers in our neighborhood lingered on the street to speak to one another, to pass along the newest stories about the horror to the south and the people who knew people who'd been inside the twin towers. Two days later the wind changed and the neighborhood smelled sharply of smoke. "I know that smell," an old man who lived in the apartment house on the corner said in accented English, and someone told me he was a Holocaust survivor.

Most nights, housebreaking the puppy we had picked up the day after our son left for school, I would run into a fireman who was heading home after working the wreckage, his eyes burning bright in a grimy face, his hands nicked and bandaged. He would pet our dog, rub her ears and muzzle, finally crouch to hold her squirmy little body close, and by the time he rose for the rest of the walk home there would be bright tear tracks in the dirt on his face. I tried not to cry until he was gone.

But despite the scent of death and the fighter planes flying low overhead and the interior rat-a-tat of panic and fear, there was also that hidden gratitude, the feeling on the part of most New Yorkers that they might have been downtown, that they could have gone to a meeting or a breakfast, that they somehow were still alive. For me that gratitude was also professional. The morning of September 12, 2001, I was at my desk first thing, no preliminaries, no computer games, seizing the chance to write about an event more destructive, more transformative, and more important than any I had ever written about during three decades as a journalist. And at that moment I thanked God, not only for the safety of my family and friends, but for the gift of being permitted to do what I do for a living.

It's a strange job, covering and commenting on the news. Life washes over us as it does all our fellows, and yet we see it in a completely different way than they do. Disaster, tragedy, malfeasance, change: Everything is always arranging itself into stories, making itself tidy and suitable for 900-word retellings. Nothing is too messy to be summed up in a headline or a sound bite. We are the people who go to wars with laptops instead of guns, who look at the scene of the crime without turning away, who stand in the flickering heat of a house fire and take down the details as someone jumps from a third-story window. We ask questions ordinary people would be ashamed to ask. We watch. That is our job.

The greater the event, the larger the disconnect between what we feel as human beings and how we look at things dispassionately as reporters. I remember well arriving back in the city in 1977 after telling our families that we had become engaged and emerging from the Holland Tunnel, not into the twinkle glare of the downtown streets but into darkness limned with the foreboding shadows of buildings black-on-black, New York City absent all electrical power. For just an instant I thought how amazingly different the place looked, how bright the stars, how dark the streets. But almost immediately everything coalesced into a single thought: how big the story!

I do not know any reporter who truly managed to feel that way about the events of September 11, although all of us knew it was indeed the biggest story we would ever cover. It was also the one in which the human part of us stayed in the forefront, right there beside the notebook. The pain was too great, the loss too enormous, the shock too overwhelming. Most of my colleagues stayed whole during the days that followed, feeling the event and covering it at the same time. This is relatively rare but, in this case, absolutely necessary, not only, I think, for the mental health of the reporters but for the verisimilitude of the stories they produced. I have never been quite as proud of being in the business as I was during those dreadful days, when newspapers, magazines, and television all produced exemplary work. In the aftermath of the terrorist attacks, *The New York Times* would win more Pulitzers than it ever had, and *Newsweek* would be honored with the National Magazine Award for best magazine in its circulation class. This was no accident. The story of what happened to the people in those buildings and to the United States was so enormous that it called upon the best within all of us to respond. Some people did that by combing the wreckage, cooking for the rescue crews, setting up funds for widows and orphans. In my business we did it by writing the truth, beautifully.

For me personally the opportunity to do this was something of an accident of timing. I had been in the newspaper business for many years, as a reporter, an editor, and finally a columnist, and while I had loved it almost insanely, I had always hoped someday to write novels. I'd managed to work on my fiction while I was a columnist, but eventually the challenge of keeping on top of the news and on top of three young children and ricocheting wildly between the two while trying to live in the invented world of fiction became too much for me. In 1995 I left *The New York Times* and, I thought, the world of journalism for good. One of the most enduring memories of my life will be walking my last night down Forty-third Street, past the *New York Times* building, the globe lamps with the old English logo glowing black against the white light. I felt as though a door had slammed at my back, and while I'd blown it shut myself, it was still not a good feeling.

For the first year I was a recovering journalist, not a recovered one. Occasionally news would break out and I would feel a frisson, like a phantom limb: I know about that! I have some thoughts! And once one of the children, in that inimitable way children have, went to the heart of it when we were watching the report of a doctor murdered at an abortion clinic. "Who's going to write about this stuff now that you're gone?" he said, chewing thoughtfully on a Fruit Roll-Up.

But the children also agreed that what they called "that look" had disappeared. I had not even known that there was a particular look, but when they reprised the semiconscious mother of seasons past it turned out to be the look a woman might have while listening to an account of a bad call at a basketball game or a hilarious episode of flatulence in the fifth-grade classroom while simultaneously thinking of welfare reform or gun control. According to their reports, I now appeared to be attending at least some of the time. Certainly it had become easier to attend to the business of writing fiction, and I found myself inhabiting the world of my third novel in a way that had been more difficult to do with the two before it, falling in and not climbing out every other day for a visit to a homeless shelter or a wild six hours banging out a screed on capital punishment. It was a good life, and whenever I was asked whether I missed being a journalist, I always answered, "No."

But five years into it the editor in chief at *Newsweek* had offered me a prime piece of real estate, the back page of the magazine and its venerable "Last Word" column. My essays would run only every other week, which left plenty of time to wallow in the invented world of a new novel. The first column was like riding the proverbial bicycle; you may be shaky, but you never forget. I was nearly two years into the routine when the worst happened that September morning and terrorists flew planes into the World Trade Center, the Pentagon, and, because of the intervention of a group of heroic passengers, an empty field in Pennsylvania. And at that moment I was so glad to have a column that I could have written one every day. I looked time and time again at my son's message: I NEED TO HEAR YOUR VOICE.

It was not that I necessarily had something distinctive to say about the savagery of the terrorists, the scope of the devastation, or the psychological scars left on the nation, although that was what I tried to produce in the long run-up to the first anniversary of the attack. I wanted to serve the readers; I also wanted to serve myself, to understand for my own sake as well as theirs. That I have always done through the algebra of prose—this word, to this one, and so on, and so on, until by inches an idea is born, and sometimes even an epiphany. That is one of the things journalists do when they go about their work, one of the collateral benefits of our hit-and-run lives. We learn to understand the world, what is important and what is important to us, and therefore who we truly are. The great plagiarism scandals in the profession have always originated with people who are empty vessels and are therefore comfortable filling the emptiness with invention, which is a fancy way of saying lies. Real reporters are always searching for some version of the truth so that, in the long run, they can assemble the truth about the world out of all the stories they have covered and the things they have learned. That is why, in contrast to the common belief that they are the world's great cynics, the best journalists are the world's great idealists. They have experienced firsthand the great soothing balance of human existence. For every disgrace there is a triumph, for every wrong there is a moment of justice, for every funeral a wedding, for every obituary a birth announcement.

There was no better time to be about this work than on September 11, 2001, and not because it was what we like to call a great story. It transcended that, as it transcended so much else we had ever imagined or known. But to try to cast light into the gray darkness that fell as those buildings burned and fell to bits was a uniquely important undertaking that I would not have wanted to watch from the sidelines. And it cemented what I had always known about the business, that it had the ability to make you better than you thought you could be because of the ordinary courage you saw at every turn.

Two nights after the terrorist attacks I was driving home from New Jersey, where I had given a speech, and as I came around the ramp that leads to the Lincoln Tunnel I saw across the river a great plume of gray smoke with orange fire at its center, a hellish foundry where two of the city's greatest landmarks had stood just days before. The man driving the car and I both let out a kind of strangled sound, a gasp and a cry together, and both of us wept. "God help us," he said. And as he did I took a notebook from my bag and wrote down what he said and how it looked and how I felt.

1 Heart

PERHAPS IT WAS INEVITABLE that we'd wind up with a couple of second-generation writers around the house. All three children had grown up thinking being a writer was as easy as going upstairs and then coming down to get a Diet Coke, muttering "I should have gone to med school." One afternoon I was talking to one of them about what he saw as the trajectory of his future career as a fiction writer—I believe the term "working construction" came up more than once—when he shrugged and said, "I guess I'll start with a thinly veiled semiautobiographical novel."

It's no more than I deserve. I've been writing about my children since there were children to write about. And I'll say about it the same thing I said to the guy who called in to a Chicago radio station and complained that I was opinionated: That's what I'm paid for. During one period of my life my job was to write a column in which the kids provided most of my material, mainly because I had two under the age of two and I didn't get out of the house enough to have anything else to write about. What saved me was the fact that a lot of that material was universal, at least among women of a certain age. So universal, in fact, that the paper once heard from a real nutbar who insisted that I was plagiarizing my column from the contents of her journals. She, too, had little boys who played with Legos and sometimes misfired when they stood in front of the toilet.

There are various criticisms of writing about your own kids: It's too cute, or it's not illuminating, or it's downright exploitative. I ran all of them through what was left of my mind in those years, while I was watching Christmas pageants with toddler sheep and attending parties at which at least half the guests had a major emotional break somewhere between the cake and the presents. And if really pushed I would have had an unsatisfactory answer for why I did it: For the moment, it was my beat.

But in retrospect I think I was being a little too apologetic about the entire business. The world of children and child-rearing is social history writ small but indelible, whether it's the minutiae of Barbie dolls and Power Ranger action figures or the phenomenon of books like *Harry Potter* or *The Cat in the Hat*. It's a shared experience, not just for the children but for their parents, and a snapshot of where we were then.

And it inevitably leads you to write about other people's kids as well, the ones who get in trouble, who die too young, who live hopeless lives in places your lucky semiautobiographical types will never live and maybe never visit. If the job of a good reporter is, as H. L. Mencken once said, "to afflict the comfortable and comfort the afflicted," then you can easily do both at once by writing about how tough society can be on its youngest members. And to the extent that you can make two people who care more than anything in the world about one small child thereby generalize their concerns to other small children, that feels like a very good thing.

At a certain point I traded writing about my own kids for writing about the troubles of kids in general. Plumbing the lives of the ones you live with every day has a fairly short shelf life if you know what you're doing as a parent. You have to be more careful as they become more conscious and more literate. But there comes a time when even taking care is not enough, and an absolute ban on the territory is clearly in order. No teenager I have ever known wants to read in a newspaper or magazine about that little sex talk you decided to have one night after he came home with a hickey. ("The only sexual behavior that doesn't survive high school," says my friend Gail, who is my mother role model and stays calm about everything.) Actually, no teenager really wants to have the little sex talk, so having it memorialized in print, for everyone else's parents to see—"Oh, I see Maria and her mom had a very serious discussion the other day"—only adds insult to injury. And puberty.

On the other hand, putting it all down in sentence form makes it easier to go back and look with a gimlet eye at the early years in a way most of us are unwilling to do when the children are small, especially when bystanders keep insisting we must be engaged in an enterprise of unwavering joy even though a fair amount of that enterprise consists of disposing of waste products. There is only one column I have ever written under duress; it came after a woman in Texas had drowned all five of her young children while in the grip of postpartum depression. My editor insisted, and he was right. After many years of hearing nightmare tales of children who did not sleep through the night until they approached adolescence (when of course they began sleeping through the afternoon), I became aware that the universe had arranged for me to have a pretty easy run as a mother. But even an easy time can be hard, and so there's probably no other issue that demands real honesty as much as motherhood does. (It may also be the only emotional role in which it is possible to be honest and balanced at the same time. Writers are wont to rip the lid off the institution of marriage once divorced, but they wind up telling only part of the story. Usually the bad part.) I tried to be honest, perhaps painfully so, in the wake of that shocking act of multiple infanticide, and you could tell how seldom that happened by the reader reaction to the resulting column about the demands of child-rearing. "Thank God" was the prevailing sentiment from women who felt as though they'd checked their selves at the labor room door. I was once one of them, but I got lucky in a big way. I got to write about it.

Now most of what goes on in my children's lives becomes grist for their own mills, episodes in their own essays and stories. Times come, times go. Once I knew every episode of *Ren & Stimpy;* once I foraged desperately for the Christmas toy you could never manage to score, the one that was featured on the news with parents in sleeping bags waiting for Toys "R" Us to open, be it for Power Rangers or Furbys or Boglins. The parade has passed me by. I have never watched *SpongeBob SquarePants* and the Christmas list is heavy on Tower Records and J.Crew clothes. Someday I will return to writing about these children, but only when they are adults and can fight back properly in print if they so choose. The weddings, perhaps. The job searches. Maybe the grandchildren. And when that semiautobiographical novel appears—oh, I am so there.

Good-bye Dr. Spock

NOVEMBER 2000

IF NOT FOR THE PHOTOGRAPHS I might have a hard time believing they ever existed. The pensive infant with the swipe of
dark bangs and the black button eyes of a Raggedy Andy doll.
The placid baby with the yellow ringlets and the high piping
voice. The sturdy toddler with the lower lip that curled into an
apostrophe above her chin.

All my babies are gone now. I say this not in sorrow but in dis-
belief. I take great satisfaction in what I have today: three almost
adults, two taller than me, one closing in fast. Three people who
read the same books I do and have learned not to be afraid of dis-
agreeing with me in their opinion of them, who sometimes tell
vulgar jokes that make me laugh until I choke and cry, who need
razor blades and shower gel and privacy, who want to keep their
doors closed more than I like. Who, miraculously, go to the bathroom, zip up their jackets, and move food from plate to mouth all
by themselves. Like the trick soap I bought for the bathroom with

a rubber ducky at its center, the baby is buried deep within each, barely discernible except through the unreliable haze of the past.

Everything in all the books I once pored over is finished for me now. Penelope Leach. Berry Brazelton. Dr. Spock. The ones on sibling rivalry and sleeping through the night and early childhood education, all grown obsolete. Along with *Goodnight Moon* and *Where the Wild Things Are,* they are battered, spotted, well used. But I suspect that if you flipped the pages, dust would rise like memories.

What those books taught me, finally, and what the women on the playground taught me, and the well-meaning relations and the older parents at cocktail parties—what they taught me was that they couldn't really teach me very much at all. Raising children is presented at first as a true-false test, then becomes multiple choice, until finally, far along, you realize that it is an endless essay. No one knows anything. One child responds well to positive reinforcement, another can only be managed with a stern voice and a time-out. One boy is toilet trained at three, his brother at two. When my first child was born, parents were told to put baby to bed on his belly so that he would not choke on his own spit-up. By the time my last arrived, babies were put down on their backs because of research on sudden infant death syndrome.

As a new parent this ever-shifting certainty is terrifying, and then soothing. Eventually you must learn to trust yourself. Eventually the research will follow. First science told us they were insensate blobs. But we thought they were looking, and watching, and learning, even when they spent so much time hitting themselves in the face. And eventually science said that we were right, that important cognitive function began in early babyhood. First science said they should be put on a feeding schedule. But sometimes they seemed hungry in two hours, sometimes three, sometimes all the time, so that we never even bothered to button up. And eventually science said that that was right, and that they would be best fed on demand. First science said environment was the great shaper of human nature. But it certainly seemed as though those babies had distinct personalities, some contemplative, some gregarious, some crabby. And eventually science said that was right, too, and that they were hardwired exactly as we had suspected.

Still, the temptation to defer to the experts was huge. The literate parent, who approaches everything—cooking, decorating, life—as though there was a paper due or an exam scheduled is in particular peril when the kids arrive. How silly it all seems now, obsessing about language acquisition and physical milestones, riding the waves of normal, gifted, hyperactive, all those labels that reduced individuality to a series of cubbyholes. But I could not help myself. I had watched my mother casually raise five children born over ten years, but by watching her I intuitively knew that I was engaged in the greatest—and potentially most catastrophic—task of my life. I knew that there were mothers who had worried with good reason, that there were children who would have great challenges to meet. We were lucky; ours were not among them. Nothing horrible or astonishing happened: There was hernia surgery, some stitches, a broken arm and a fuchsia cast to go with it.

Mostly ours were the ordinary everyday terrors and miracles of raising a child, and our children's challenges the old familiar ones of learning to live as themselves in the world. The trick was to get past my fears, my ego, and my inadequacies to help them do that. During my first pregnancy I picked up a set of lovely old clothbound books at a flea market. Published in 1933, they were called *Mother's Encyclopedia,* and one volume described what a mother needs to be: "psychologically good: sound, wholesome, healthy, unafraid, able to deal with the world and to live in this particular age, an integrated personality, an adjusted person." In a word, yow.

It is good that we know so much more now, know that mothers need not be perfect to be successful. But some of what we learn is as pernicious as that daunting description, calculated to make us feel like failures every single day. I remember fifteen years ago poring over one of Dr. Brazelton's wonderful books on child development, in which he describes three different sorts of infants: average, quiet, and active. I was looking for a sub-quiet codicil (see: slug) for an eighteen-month-old who did not walk. Was there something wrong with his fat little legs? Was there something wrong with his tiny little mind? Was he developmentally delayed, physically challenged? Was I insane? Last year he went to China. Next year he goes to college. He can walk just fine. He can walk too well. Every part of raising children at some point comes down to this: Be careful what you wish for.

Every part of raising children is humbling, too. Believe me, mistakes were made. They have all been enshrined in the "Remember When Mom Did" Hall of Fame. The outbursts, the temper tantrums, the bad language—mine, not theirs. The times the baby fell off the bed. The times I arrived late for preschool pickup. The nightmare sleepover. The horrible summer camp. The day when the youngest came barreling out of the classroom with a 98 on her geography test, and I responded, "What did you get wrong?" (She insisted I include that.) The time I ordered food at the McDonald's drive-through speaker and then drove away without picking it up from the window. (They all insisted I include that.) I did not allow them to watch *The Simpsons* for the first two seasons. What was I thinking?

But the biggest mistake I made is the one that most of us make while doing this. I did not live in the moment enough. This is particularly clear now that the moment is gone, captured only in photographs. There is one picture of the three of them sitting in the grass on a quilt in the shadow of the swing set on a summer day, ages six, four, and one. And I wish I could remember what we ate, and what we talked about, and how they sounded, and how they looked when they slept that night. I wish I had not been in such a hurry to get on to the next thing: dinner, bath, book, bed. I wish I had treasured the doing a little more and the getting it done a little less.

Even today I'm not sure what worked and what didn't, what was me and what was simply life. How much influence did I really have over the personality of the former baby who cried only when we gave parties and who today, as a teenager, still dislikes socializing and crowds? When they were very small I suppose I thought someday they would become who they were because of what I'd done. Now I suspect they simply grew into their true selves because they demanded in a thousand ways that I back off and let them be.

There was babbling I forgot to do, stimulation they never got, foods I meant to introduce and never got around to introducing. If a black-and-white mobile really increases depth perception and early exposure to classical music increases the likelihood of perfect pitch, I blew it. The books said to be relaxed and I was often tense, matter-of-fact, and I was sometimes over-the-top. And look how it all turned out. I wound up with the three people I like best in the world, who have done more than anyone to excavate my essential humanity. That's what the books never told me. I was bound and determined to learn from the experts. It just took me a while to figure out who the experts were.

Our Tired,
Our Poor, Our Kids

MARCH 2001

SIX PEOPLE LIVE HERE, in a room the size of the master bedroom in a modest suburban house. Trundles, bunk beds, dressers side by side stacked with toys, clothes, boxes, in tidy claustrophobic clutter. One woman, five children. The baby was born in a shelter. The older kids can't wait to get out of this one. Everyone gets up at 6:00 A.M., the little ones to go to day care, the others to school. Their mother goes out to look for an apartment when she's not going to drug treatment meetings. "For what they pay for me to stay in a shelter I could have lived in the Hamptons," Sharanda says.

Here is the parallel universe that has flourished while the more fortunate were rewarding themselves for the stock split with SUVs and home additions. There is a boom market in homelessness. But these are not the men on the streets of San Francisco holding out cardboard signs to the tourists. They are children, hundreds of thousands of them, twice as likely to repeat a grade or be hospitalized and four times as likely to go hungry as the kids with a roof over their heads. Twenty years ago New York City provided emergency shelter for just under a thousand families a day; last month it had to find spaces for ten thousand children on a given night. Not since the Great Depression have this many babies, toddlers, and kids had no place like home.

Three mothers sit in the living room of a temporary residence called Casa Rita in the Bronx and speak of this in the argot of poverty. "The landlord don't call back when they hear you got EARP," says Rosie, EARP being the Emergency Assistance Rehousing Program. "You get priority for Section Eight if you're in a shelter," says Edna, which means federal housing programs will put you higher on the list. Edna has four kids, three in foster care; she arrived at Casa Rita, she says, "with two bags and a baby." Rosie has three; they share a bathroom down the hall with two other families. Sharanda's five range in age from thirteen to just over a year. Her eldest was put in the wrong grade when he changed schools. "He's humiliated, living here," his mother says.

All three are anxious to move on, although they appreciate this place, where they can get shelter, get sober, and keep their kids at the same time. They remember the Emergency Assistance Unit, the city office that is the gateway to the system, where hundreds of families sit every day surrounded by their bags, where children sleep on benches until they are shuffled off dull-eyed for one night in a shelter or a motel, only to return as supplicants again the next day.

In another world, middle-class Americans have embraced new home starts, the stock market, and the Gap. But in the world of these displaced families, problems ignored or fumbled or unforeseen during this great period of prosperity have dovetailed into an enormous subculture of children who think that only rich people have their own bedrooms. Twenty years ago, when the story of the homeless in America became a staple of news reporting, the solution was presented as a simple one: affordable housing. Last year the Low Income Housing Coalition calculated that the hourly salary necessary to afford the average two-bedroom apartment was around $12. That's more than twice the minimum wage.

The result is that in many cities police officers and teachers cannot afford to live where they work, that in Las Vegas old motels provide housing for casino employees, that in shelters now there is a contingent of working poor who get up off their cots and go off to their jobs. The result is that if you are evicted for falling behind on your rent, if there is a bureaucratic foul-up in your welfare check or the factory in which you work shuts down, the chances of finding another place to live are very small indeed. You're one understanding relative, one paycheck, one second chance from the street. And so are your kids.

So-called welfare reform, which emphasizes cutbacks and make-work, has played a part in all this. A study done in San Diego in 1998 found that a third of homeless families had recently had benefits terminated or reduced, and that most said that was how they had wound up on the street. Drugs, alcohol, and domestic abuse also land mothers with kids in the shelter system or lead them to hand their children over to relatives or foster homes. Today the average homeless woman is younger than ever before, may have been in foster care or in shelters herself, and so considers a chaotic childhood the norm. Many never finished high school and have never held a job.

Ralph Nunez, who runs the organization Homes for the Homeless, says that all this calls for new attitudes. "People don't like to hear it, but shelters are going to be the low-income housing of the future," he says. "So how do we enrich the experience and use the system to provide job training and education?" Bonnie Stone of Women In Need, which has eight other residences along with Casa Rita, says, "We're pouring everything we've got into the nine months most of them are here—nutrition, treatment, budgeting. By the time they leave they have a subsidized apartment, day care, and hopefully some life skills they didn't have before."

But these organizations are rafts in a rising river of need that has roared through this country without most of us ever even knowing. So now you know. There are hundreds of thousands of little nomads in America, sleeping in the backs of cars, on floors in welfare offices, or in shelters five to a room. What would it mean to spend your childhood drifting from one strange bed to another, waking in the morning to try to figure out where you'd landed today, without those things that confer security and happiness: a familiar picture on the wall, a certain slant of light through a curtained window? "Give me your tired, your poor," it says on the base of the Statue of Liberty, to welcome foreigners. Oh, but they are already here, the small refugees from the ruin of the American dream, even if you cannot see them.

Doing Nothing
Is Something

MAY 2002

SUMMER IS COMING SOON. I can feel it in the softening of the air but I can see it, too, in the textbooks on my children's desks. The number of uncut pages at the back grows smaller and smaller. The loose-leaf is ragged at the edges, the binder plastic ripped at the corner. An old remembered glee rises inside me. Summer is coming. Uniform skirts in mothballs. Pencils with their points left broken. Open windows. Day trips to the beach. Pickup games. Hanging out.

How boring it was.

Of course, it was the making of me, as a human being and a writer. Downtime is where we become ourselves, looking into the middle distance, kicking at the curb, lying on the grass or sitting on the stoop and staring at the tedious blue of the summer sky. I don't believe you can write poetry, or compose music, or become an actor without downtime, and plenty of it, a hiatus that passes for boredom but is really the quiet moving of the wheels inside that fuel creativity.

And that, to me, is one of the saddest things about the lives of American children today. Soccer leagues, acting classes, tutors—the calendar of the average middle-class kid is so over-the-top that soon PalmPilots will be sold in Toys "R" Us. Our children are as overscheduled as we are, and that is saying something.

This has become so bad that parents have arranged to schedule times for unscheduled time. Earlier this year the privileged suburb of Ridgewood, New Jersey, announced a Family Night, when there would be no homework, no athletic practices, and no after-school events. This was terribly exciting until I realized that this was not one night a week, but one single night. There is even a free-time movement and website: Family Life 1st. Among the frequently asked questions provided online: "What would families do with family time if they took it back?"

Let me make a suggestion for the kids involved: How about nothing? It is not simply that it is pathetic to consider the lives of children who don't have a moment between piano and dance and homework to talk about their day or just search for split ends, an enormously satisfying leisure-time activity of my youth. There is also ample psychological research suggesting that what we might call "doing nothing" is when human beings actually do their best thinking, and when creativity comes to call. Perhaps we are creating an entire generation of people whose ability to think outside the box, as the current parlance of business has it, is being systematically stunted by scheduling.

A study by the University of Michigan quantified the downtime deficit; in the last twenty years American kids have lost about four unstructured hours a week. There has even arisen a global Right to Play movement: In the Third World it is often about child labor, but in the United States it is about the sheer labor of being a perpetually busy child. In Omaha a group of parents recently lobbied for additional recess. Hooray, and yikes.

How did this happen? Adults did it. There is a culture of adult distrust that suggests that a kid who is not playing softball or attending science-enrichment programs—or both—is huffing or boosting cars: If kids are left alone, they will not stare into the middle distance and consider the meaning of life and how come your nose in pictures never looks the way you think it should, but instead will get into trouble. There is also the culture of cutthroat and unquestioning competition that leads even the parents of preschoolers to gab about prestigious colleges without a trace of irony: This suggests that any class in which you do not enroll your first grader will put him at a disadvantage in, say, law school.

Finally, there is a culture of workplace presence (as opposed to productivity). Try as we might to suggest that all these enrichment activities are for the good of the kid, there is ample evidence that they are really for the convenience of parents with way too little leisure time of their own. Stories about the resignation of presidential aide Karen Hughes unfailingly reported her dedication to family time by noting that she arranged to get home at 5:30 one night a week to have dinner with her son. If one weekday dinner out of five is considered laudable, what does that say about what's become normative?

Summer is coming. It used to be a time apart for kids, a respite from the clock and the copybook, the organized day. Every once in a while, either guilty or overwhelmed or tired of listening to me keen about my monumental boredom, my mother would send me to some rinky-dink park program that consisted almost entirely of three-legged races and making things out of Popsicle sticks. Instead now there are music camps, sports camps, fat camps, probably thin camps. I mourn hanging out in the backyard. I mourn playing Wiffle ball in the street without a sponsor and matching shirts. I mourn drawing in the dirt with a stick.

Maybe that kind of summer is gone for good. Maybe this is the leading edge of a new way of living that not only has no room for contemplation but is contemptuous of it. But if downtime cannot be squeezed during the school year into the life of frantic and often joyless activity with which our children are saddled while their parents pursue frantic and often joyless activity of their own, what about summer? Do most adults really want to stand in line for Space Mountain or sit in traffic to get to a shore house that doesn't have enough saucepans? Might it be even more enriching for their children to stay at home and do nothing? For those who say they will only watch TV or play on the computer, a piece of technical advice: The cable box can be unhooked, the modem removed. Perhaps it is not too late for American kids to be given the gift of enforced boredom for at least a week or two, staring into space, bored out of their gourds, exploring the inside of their own heads. "To contemplate is to toil, to think is to do," said Victor Hugo. "Go outside and play," said Prudence Quindlen. Both of them were right.

No Privilege
for Parents

JANUARY 2000

THE SUPREME COURT WAS PREPARING to extend the evidentiary doctor-patient privilege to social workers practicing psychotherapy, and Justice Scalia was, as usual, dissenting. "Ask the average citizen: would your mental health be more significantly impaired by preventing you from seeing a psychotherapist, or by preventing you from getting advice from your mom," he wrote. "I have little doubt what the answer would be. Yet there is no mother-child privilege."

And there, in that last sentence, lies a tale of public ignorance, judicial conservatism, and legislative stalemate, a tale that would do well to end where we just began: in the halls of the country's highest court.

"The law," as Mr. Bumble so pithily observes in *Oliver Twist*, "is a ass." The absence of the *n* in that sentence is glaring, but not so glaring as the absence of the privilege Justice Scalia mentioned in his opinion. While the United States counts as commonplace privilege between attorney and client, priest and penitent, doctor and patient, and, of course, husband and wife, there is no generally accepted protection for parent and child that considers their conversations as confidential and not open to routine courtroom scrutiny. Parents can be compelled to testify against their child, children to testify against their parents. The end result is this: If your teenage son has done something wrong, he can talk to a lawyer, a minister, a pediatrician, or a therapist with some confidence that they will not be obliged to repeat what he has said to a grand jury or on the witness stand.

You, on the other hand, might be well advised to raise your hand and say, "Son, don't say a thing or it could be used against you."

All the prosecutors out there scoff as one, because the prosecutorial response to this issue is that district attorneys, being frequently parents themselves, and often human beings, would not ask a mother to drop a dime on her daughter, or a son to rat out his dad. (This is made to sound high-minded, when in fact it is often expedient; juries don't like the idea, and juries must be kept happy.) But the insistence that parent and child are rarely asked to give evidence against one another has become increasingly lame in light of the high-profile cases of recent years. Monica Lewinsky's mother, looking like she was ready to keel over, was hustled into court in Washington, and the parents of Amy Grossberg, accused of killing her newborn son, were subpoenaed in Delaware.

Many foreign countries recognize the legal sanctity of what may be the most sacred of all relationships, and three states have passed limited parent-child privilege statutes, although each is in some way unsatisfactory. The Lewinsky matter led members of Congress to propose legislation, but so far it has gone exactly nowhere. "In this day and age anything that seems to limit prosecutors is unlikely to get very far," says Lawrence Goldman, who once drafted a parent-child rule for the National Association of Criminal Defense Lawyers. The Third Circuit Court of Appeals agreed not long ago to hear the case of a retired FBI agent who balked at testifying to a grand jury about conversations with his eighteen-year-old son. Unfortunately the appellate panel ruled against him, but not before its only female justice, Carol Mansmann, had written an eloquent dissent, tracing the right of parent-child privilege to ancient Roman and Jewish laws. "The protection of strong and trusting parent-child relationships outweighs the government's interest in disclosure," Judge Mansmann wrote.

That's it in a legal nutshell, but an added civilian perspective might be this: The lack of the privilege is illogical, and defies both common sense and the public weal. In today's atmosphere of easy divorce, perhaps even since the first infant smiled up glassy-eyed at her mother, the ties of parenthood often trump those of matrimony. If spousal privilege is taken for granted, how can there be no similar protection of communications between parent and child? It seems so obvious that I would daresay many Americans believe it already exists. Of course, even for those who understand there is no such protection, it is a rare parent who would inhibit confidences from a child because they feared a future subpoena or lawsuit. "Kids trust their parents, and parents protect their kids," says Catherine Ross, an associate professor of law at George Washington University who is in favor of the establishment of a parent-child privilege. "That's the way it is. That's the way it ought to be. By creating the privilege we're in effect legitimizing a preexisting condition."

By not creating it, we're suborning perjury. I would be fully prepared to lie under oath if I considered it to be the best thing for my kid, and I would consider that a more moral position than telling the truth. And I am certain I am in the majority. Yet each time a parent says to a troubled or confused kid, "You can tell me anything," there is a covert, perhaps unwitting lie at the center of the vow. That's untenable.

In the years to come the issue of parent-child privilege is likely to become even more problematic and important. Frustrated by school shootings and adolescent criminality, states are embracing parental responsibility statutes that hold adults responsible for the heinous behavior of the young. It's certain that adjudicating such cases will require parent and child to be called to testify about what they knew and when they knew it. Whatever the outcome, how will those families ever be able to trust or confide again? Will the erosion of their bond be contagious, leading each of us, little by little, to be more guarded with those we love most? Perhaps sooner or later there will be a heartbreaking case, a clear case, a case that will rise step by step to the Supreme Court. And Justice Scalia and his colleagues will consider, and reflect, what is so clearly true, both under the provisions of the law and in the high court of daily life: that the first privilege, the most compelling of them all, ought to be the one between parent and child.

In Search of a Grown-up

AUGUST 2002

A GOOD DEFENSE ATTORNEY uses what he's got, and what David Westerfield's attorney had was what is euphemistically called "lifestyle." Much of the evidence didn't look good for Westerfield as he stood trial in San Diego for the murder of a seven-year-old girl. Experts testified that little Danielle van Dam's fingerprints and hair were found in the RV he took into the desert the weekend she disappeared and that her blood was found on a jacket he brought to the dry cleaner first thing Monday morning.

So Westerfield's lawyer tried to counter that forensics mess with another sort of mess, the messy lifestyle of Danielle's mom and dad. It was a little difficult to keep it all straight, but it seems as if Damon van Dam had had sex, in the presence of assorted spouses, with both of the women with whom his wife, Brenda, went out drinking on the night that their little girl went missing. That night the women smoked marijuana in a garage fitted with a special lock intended to keep the kids from barging in, then went out to a bar for an evening of heavy drinking and dirty dancing, then came back to the home, where Damon made out with one of his wife's friends until Brenda told him that it was rude to do so because they had guests downstairs, a rule of etiquette with which I was not familiar.

Counsel never succeeded in making this relevant to the question of who took Danielle from her pink-and-purple bedroom and dumped her body in the desert, where it was found, badly decomposed, nearly a month later.

But it does have something to do with a curious attitude that seems to have taken root among some modern parents. And that is that life with kids is just like life without kids, only with bunk beds.

It is possible to have children and still work punishing hours. It is possible to have children and still have a bitchen social life. It is possible to have children and still booze it up and do drugs, just like you did when you were young and single.

It is possible. It is surely not desirable.

Having children changes everything. There's constant grousing about the failure of various sports figures to serve as national role models, when all they really are qualified to do is pass a little ball around a little area. But the moment that little cord gets cut with those little scissors, two little people have been turned into role models instantly, whether they like it or not.

Everything afterward is a process of compromise and even self-sacrifice, or ought to be. The center has shifted, from sleeping late and midnight movies to Saturday soccer games and those night terrors that lead to three in a bed, two of them exhausted. This can all be onerous. Clean up your language. Clean up your act. Cut down on the business trips, the profanity, and the beer.

"An inadvertent example" is how the psychologist Lawrence Balter describes what a parent becomes without even trying. A child is watching. And judging. And learning, always learning.

Or sometimes people behave exactly as before. Nothing inside them is essentially different; otherwise they would not forget and leave the baby in the car to suffocate in the heat while they go off to work—or the hairdresser. Alongside the oft-invoked plight of teenage parents, we have the unspoken plight of the kids of parents who act as if they're still teenagers themselves. The saddest shows on trash-talk TV are ones like "My Mom Dresses Too Sexy." If you feel the need to put a lock on the garage to keep your kids from walking in while you smoke marijuana, it may be nature's way of telling you the time to drop the bong is when you put up the crib.

To much fanfare Sylvia Ann Hewlett published an account earlier this year of how high-achieving professional women found themselves successful and childless. Many of them seemed to have missed the basic biological lesson that fertility declines sharply with age. And some of them seem to have bought into a mathematical impossibility: that there are an endless number of hours in any day, and that devoting most of them to work would still result in sufficient hours available for child-rearing. Lots of people have bought into this cockamamy equation, although simple common sense says that it just won't work. Something's got to give, and that something is you.

It is possible to feel deep sympathy for Brenda and Damon van Dam's loss, and yet at the same time to think that they missed something basic about the way a person ought to modify their behavior when elevated to the position of parent. They loved and lost their daughter in the kind of Southern California neighborhood immortalized in the movie *Poltergeist,* in which each spanking new house without a history looks so much like its fellows that you wonder how anyone recognizes his own. But in some ways they are no different from many in other settings all over the country. Is it the youth culture that suggested that no one really had to play the role of grown-up in the morality play that is life? Instead there is a thriving subculture of parents who act as if everything goes on as before. That's ridiculous. Having kids changes everything. Or at least it ought to.

Playing God
on No Sleep

JULY 2001

SO A WOMAN WALKS INTO a pediatrician's office. She's tired, she's hot, and she's been up all night throwing sheets into the washer because the smaller of the two boys has projectile vomiting so severe it looks like a special effect from *The Exorcist*. Oh, and she's nauseous, too, because since she already has two kids under the age of four it made perfect sense to have another, and she's four months pregnant. In the doctor's waiting room, which sounds like a cross between an orchestra tuning loudly and a 747 taking off, there is a cross-stitched sampler on the wall. It says GOD COULD NOT BE EVERYWHERE SO HE MADE MOTHERS.

This is not a joke and that is not the punch line. Or maybe it is. The woman was me, the sampler real, and the sentiments it evoked unforgettable: incredulity, disgust, and that out-of-body feeling that is the corollary of sleep deprivation and adrenaline rush, with a soupçon of shoulder barf thrown in. I kept reliving this moment, and others like it, as I read with horrified fascination the story of Andrea Yates, a onetime nurse suffering from postpartum depression who apparently spent a recent morning drowning her five children in the bathtub. There is a part of my mind that imagines the baby, her starfish hands pink beneath the water, or the biggest boy fighting back, all wiry arms and legs, and then veers sharply away, aghast, appalled.

But there's another part of my mind, the part that remembers the end of a day in which the milk spilled phone rang one cried another hit a fever rose the medicine gone the car sputtered another cried the cable out *Sesame Street* gone all cried stomach upset full diaper no more diapers Mommy I want water Mommy my throat hurts Mommy I don't feel good. Every mother I've asked about the Yates case has the same reaction. She's appalled; she's aghast. And then she gets this look. And the look says that at some forbidden level she understands. The look says that there are two very different kinds of horror here. There is the unimaginable idea of the killings. And then there is the entirely imaginable idea of going quietly bonkers in a house with five kids under the age of seven.

The insidious cult of motherhood is summed up by the psychic weight of the sampler on that doctor's wall. We are meant to be all things to small people, surrounded by bromides and soppy verse and smiling strangers who talk about how lucky we are. And we are lucky. My children have been the making of me as a human being, which does not mean they have not sometimes been an overwhelming and mind-boggling responsibility. That last is the love that dare not speak its name, the love that is fraught with fear and fatigue and inevitable resentment. But between the women who cannot have children and sometimes stare at our double strollers grief-stricken and the grandmothers who make raising eight or ten sound like a snap and insist we micromanage and overanalyze, there is no leave to talk about the dark side of being a surrogate deity, omniscient and out of milk all at the same time.

The weight was not always so heavy. Once the responsibility was spread around extended families, even entire towns. The sociologist Jessie Bernard has this to say:

> The way we institutionalize motherhood in our society—assigning sole responsibility for child care to the mother, cutting her off from the easy help of others in an isolated household, requiring round-the-clock tender loving care, and making such care her exclusive activity—is not only new and unique, but not even a good way for either women or—if we accept as a criterion the amount of maternal warmth shown—for children. It may in fact be the worst.

It has gotten no better since those words were written twenty-five years ago. Women not working outside their homes feel compelled to make their job inside it seem both weighty and joyful; women who work outside their homes for pay feel no freedom to be ambivalent because of the sub-rosa sense that they are cutting parenting corners. All of us are caught up in a conspiracy in which we are both the conspirators and the victims of the plot. In the face of all this mythology it becomes difficult to admit that occasionally you lock yourself in the bathroom just to be alone.

The great motherhood friendships are the ones in which two women can admit this quietly to each other, over cups of tea at a table sticky with spilled apple juice and littered with markers without tops. But most of the time we keep quiet and smile. So that when someone is depressed after having a baby, when everyone is telling her that it's the happiest damn time of her life, there's no space to admit what she's really feeling. So that when someone does something as horrifying as what Andrea Yates did, there is no room for even a little bit of understanding. Yap yap yap, the world says. How could anyone do that to her children?

Well, yes. But. I'm imagining myself with five children under the age of seven, all alone after Dad goes off to work. And they're bouncing off the walls in that way little boys do, except for the baby, who needs to be fed. And fed. And fed again. And changed. The milk gets spilled. The phone rings. Mommy can I have juice? Mommy can I have lunch? Mommy can I go out back? Mommy can I come in? And I add to all that depression, mental illness, whatever was happening in that house. I'm not making excuses for Andrea Yates. I love my children more than life itself. But just because you love someone doesn't mean that taking care of them day in and day out isn't often hard, and sometimes even horrible. If God made mothers because he couldn't be everywhere, maybe he could have met us halfway and eradicated vomiting, and colic, too, and the hideous sugarcoating of what we are and what we do that leads to false cheer, easy lies, and maybe sometimes something much much worse, almost unimaginable. But not quite.

Playing Perfect
Patty-cake

APRIL 1994

WHY IN THE WORLD am I sitting here trying to recall how many hours my children spent playing with blocks when they were small? Why am I trying to tote up the time I spent reading *Pat the Bunny* versus the time that I spent wheeling them around supermarket aisles talking to myself?

Because I am looking at the study just released from the Families and Work Institute, that's why, a study that shows some day care is not as good as we might have imagined.

The assessment of family day care by the research group shows that informal care for a few children in the home of a paid provider or a family member, the most prevalent kind of child care for the small children of working mothers, is significantly flawed. Nine percent of the caregivers were rated as good quality, 56 percent adequate, and 35 percent inadequate.

Has anyone ever done a similar assessment of mothers?

That's the question we're never to ask, much less subject to prolonged scrutiny. The reason child care is such a loaded issue is that when we talk about it, we are always tacitly talking about motherhood. And when we're talking about motherhood we're always tacitly assuming that child care must be a very dim second to full-time mother care.

Which is why I'm comparing my own mothering skills with those of people who get paid for caring for kids. Do they spend more time using crayons and books than I did? Is it time to finally admit that while child care is all over the map, from stellar to deplorable, the quality of mothering can be various, too?

How well I remember, some years ago, the frisson of fear when I read that part of the evidence against Mary Beth Whitehead, in her battle to keep the child she'd conceived in a surrogate arrangement, was the testimony of a psychiatrist that she had played patty-cake incorrectly. The mother of two young children at the time, I wondered: Am I playing right?

While the Families and Work Institute study quantified the time spent in family day care in artwork, stories, puzzles, and the like, I can scarcely remember doing many of those things. But no matter; there is a clear double standard for mothers and caregivers. One mother at the park laced into a departing sitter, complaining that she'd spent all her time at the park talking to her friends while the children played nearby, oblivious to the fact that she and I were doing the same. Another once told me that she could not imagine how a family day care provider could adequately care for three small children at once, either unaware that I had three such myself or confident that mothers had magical powers.

The bar for the caregivers had been set by both of them, not at the level of our own everyday and sometimes flawed behavior but at that of some mythical being, the always child-centered and responsive mother. She is the person against whom we always measure child-care options; is it any wonder that even the good ones are often found wanting?

The truth is that the good ones are not legion, as the Families and Work Institute study suggested and the Carnegie commission noted in a blistering report on the state of America's children released this week. No one with kids would argue with the notion that more and better child-care options must be a key part of our plan for the future.

And no one will deny the special, central place parents have in the lives of their children. While the study of family day care showed that only about half the children were "securely attached" to their caregiver, studies of attachment to mothers show, happily, a much higher number.

But let's not pretend that all mothers approach their work at home joyously, competently, or well. "If you compared child-care workers against mothers, you'd probably find the same variety in quality," says Ellen Galinsky, a co-president of the Families and Work Institute.

So let's not perpetuate this cult of the perfect patty-cake mother, who renders all other options suspect and second-rate. It pits women whose children are cared for in part by others and worry that they rob them of this ideal childhood against women who care for their kids full-time and wonder why they cannot measure up to the ideal. It assumes a uniformity to our families, our kids, and our own abilities that is simply illusory. And it sets us all up for failure.

Mom Quixote

DECEMBER 1993

DAY THREE OF MY SEARCH for Mighty Morphin Power Ranger toys, and I grow weary. Sneering clerks in three stores behave as though I've asked for gold bullion when I inquire whether they have these items in stock. Driving home, I wonder whom to blame: retailers, manufacturers, or the child who waited until November to articulate a need more profound than the need for food or water. Every Christmas there is one plaything everyone desires and no one can get. Sort of like the Hope diamond. I will persevere.

Day five: Missed by minutes the unpacking of a box of Mighty Morphin Power Ranger toys at the mall. Drat these column deadlines! All were swiftly purchased by parents and (I am convinced) scalpers. My quest is complicated by the fact that I have no idea what these toys look like, since I have not yet set eyes on one. I will buy first, look later.

Day seven: "If I don't get Mighty Morphin Power Rangers, I'll know there's no Santa Claus," says the eight-year-old as he plays with his spaghetti. Back to the mall tomorrow.

Day eight: I have a vivid dream in which the Princess of Wales and I are fighting over a Mighty Morphin Power Ranger in the aisles of (I think) Harrods. "He doesn't need this," I scream, "he'll be king someday." Using her obsessively worked pectoral muscles to shove me backward, she replies, "It's not for Wills, it's for Harry." I am arrested by her security detail and taken to the Tower of London, where my son is waiting. "You didn't get them," he wails. I awaken in a cold sweat.

Day eleven: I join a group of women chatting about Mighty Morphin Power Rangers in the aisle of a Toys "R" Us. Several liken this to the Teenage Mutant Ninja Turtle mania several years ago. One woman recalls driving to Delaware to buy a Donatello. The delivery truck arrives with Mighty Maxes, X-Men, Snailiens, and Street Fighters, but no Mighty Morphin Power Rangers. One woman calls the driver a vulgar name. I buy an economy-size bag of Butterfingers and return home, disconsolate.

Day twelve: At a cocktail party I meet a woman who personally participated in the Cabbage Patch riots of 1983, sustaining a black eye while unsuccessfully fighting for a pig-faced doll with brown braids. She says her daughter is now seventeen years old and wrote a senior English essay called "Shattered Dreams" on how she felt when she did not get a Cabbage Patch doll that Christmas. "She says that's how she knew there was no Santa Claus," the woman says. My husband asks in the cab why I am so sad. I say it's the holiday spirit.

Day fifteen: I briefly consider using my influence as a member of the media to acquire Mighty Morphin Power Rangers. I muse aloud about requesting Power Rangers from the manufacturer to illustrate a story on the season's toys. My husband mentions that I have consistently refused to get tickets for opening day at Yankee Stadium under somewhat similar circumstances. Men.

Day seventeen: Preparations for the Christmas season continue apace. I am excoriated for not having a cookie cutter in the shape of Bart Simpson. Our oldest child pretends to believe in Santa Claus. His brother asks whether Santa ever runs out of toys. "Hardly ever," he replies. "What about Mighty Morphin Power Rangers?" the younger asks. "If you want Power Rangers, he'll bring Power Rangers," his brother says. I send him upstairs to study for a spelling test.

Day nineteen: *It's a Wonderful Life* is on, and I imagine my life without Mighty Morphin Power Rangers. It's better.

Day twenty: The eight-year-old talks to me while I am taking a shower. "Do you know what I am going to do on Christmas morning?" he says. "What?" I shout from the shower. "I'm going to sit all day and play with my Mighty Morphin Power Rangers," he says. "What?" I shout. When I turn off the water I see that I have forgotten to rinse the shampoo from my hair. "Do you know what?" he says as soon as I have turned the water back on. "What?" I scream. "You are the best mom in the whole wide world."

Day twenty-one: There is a shipment of Mighty Morphin Power Rangers arriving at the mall at 10:00 A.M., or at least that is what one of the sneering salesmen was overheard to say. I will be there but I cannot stay long. Drat these column deadlines! How long does it take to drive to Delaware? I will persevere.

Now It's Time for Generation Next

JANUARY 2000

HISTORY IS MOST OFTEN WRITTEN in terms of inventions and events, revolutions and revolutionary ideas. But it is always essentially the story of people. The New Deal. The new technology. Cubism. Communism. These are tales of individuals, of Roosevelt and Gates, Picasso and Castro. Biography is destiny, often for the entire world. Had Hitler been a better painter—ah, it is a conundrum for the ages.

And so I can predict this, with what I believe is considerable accuracy, about the century to come. It will be remarkable because its history will be shaped, and written, too, by a group of what promise to be remarkable human beings. The millennials, demographers have named them, born between 1977 and 1994, seventy million strong, the biggest bump in our national line graph since your parents, the baby boomers. For my money, they are a great bunch. My three, for example, are simply better than I was at their age. They are more interesting, more confident, less hidebound and uptight, better educated, more creative and, in some essential fashion, unafraid.

We, their elders, can say with pride that some of that is because of the world we have helped create, a rapidly changing world we have tried hard to embrace. One out of every seven of their peers is black, one out of every seven Latino, and because of that great diversity of population as well as greater openness at school and at home, many of them do not have the lily-white illusions that colored my insular childhood, nor some of the fears of the other that have poisoned our national discourse.

They have grown up seeing, and believing, that women are as capable as men; while at ten my career choices were either mother or Roman Catholic nun, the women of this new world have rightly convinced millennial girls that their world can be bounded by their talents and not their gender. And as they have grown to adulthood, it has become ever less necessary for gay men and lesbians to follow the old conventions of deception.

These are all good things not only because they satisfy the simple demands of justice but because tolerance has made the millennials, as a group, more tolerant of themselves, of the quirks and foibles that lead to interesting and sometimes monumental lives. It has also led many of them to be generous in ways unknown to me when I was young. In Paterson, New Jersey, nearly a third of the people working on a Habitat for Humanity building project are under twenty-five. And millennial children have grown up participating in community service programs in many of their schools as a matter of course.

As a child I remember a peculiar little philanthropy called "pagan babies," in which we Catholic school children adopted some faceless child from some foreign land, renamed her Monica or Theresa, and then showered her with nickels and quarters from our mothers' purses. By contrast my eldest son works at our church homeless shelter, with real people with whom he has a real human connection (and who get to keep their own names).

No great heroism has yet come along to define them as a group, no world war, no wrenching economic catastrophe. But they have created personal valor out of such charity. A survey last year of college freshmen, a sampling of the eldest part of the millennial curve, found that three quarters of them had done some volunteer work in the last year, at schools, in hospitals, for charities, and at church. The quality those freshmen said they admired most was integrity, and the people they admired most were their parents.

This is not the conventional wisdom about their generation. Instead their collective legacy so far is often littered with negatives, even horrors. The smaller ones are said to be spoiled, overindulged by guilty working parents, powered by the tympani of medication and video games. The teenagers are associated in the public mind with lewd music, foul mouths, and, most terrifying of all, one school shooting after another. And some of this is true. And most of it obscures the truth, particularly if you have the good fortune to know some of the millennials up close and personal.

From one generation to another, the complaint is always the same: They are not like us. This seems more obvious than ever before, looking through the long lens of the twentieth century as we leave it. Born after Watergate, Woodstock, and Vietnam, gas lines and record albums, heirs to the microchip and the cathode-ray tube, under pressure from parents who are high achievers or who wish they had been, in a world in which seemingly endless choices, good and bad, swirl around them like flakes in a snow globe: This generation lives a life that the one-size-fits-all generations before them can scarcely imagine.

I memorized the Baltimore Catechism; to this day I can tell you that God made me to know him, to love him, and to serve him in this world, and to be happy with him forever in the next. By contrast our kids and their classmates have had endless discussions about whether God exists, whether God has gender, whether a merciful God would countenance AIDS or airplane crashes.

This core generational belief, that there is usually more than one answer to any question, is threatening for their elders, raised on "because I said so." So is the fact that they are not all of a piece. The dutiful son has a pierced tongue. The student government president dresses like Morticia Addams. Where once we could identify who was who by the college, the color, the crew neck sweater, now the lines of identity are constantly blurred, in our perceptions and in the stages of their lives.

This is disconcerting, difficult, and wonderful. Socratic is better than rote. Discussion teaches more than dictums. And paths set in stone are, we've discovered, often rocky as we move along them. These are the children of peace, prosperity, and pluralism, and they have done us proud. They are the bungee-jumping generation: We could never do it ourselves, but our hearts leap and our adrenaline rises at the sight of them, arms outstretched, poised to do—what? Something wonderful. As one century changes over to another, I look out at the newest generation to come of age in this country, and I can see the future. And what I see is very very good.

Daughter of the Groom

JUNE 1993

MY FATHER WAS MARRIED for the third time last month. This makes him sound a good deal more Liz Taylorish than is accurate or fair. He is, happily, a good man who loves women and who, sadly, has had two wives die of cancer. Our eldest child wanted to tell the bride, a warm and intelligent woman we liked instantly, that there was a curse on Grandpop.

But there was a blessing on him, really, and that was that he has been able to learn from death and grief the most useful lesson they can teach, the value of life and happiness. He has taught me that, too, as he has so many other things.

I was raised as my father's oldest son. I have always known how to fish, and I have always known how to talk back. I don't know if we girls who were so raised missed out on the standard romantic attachment to our fathers, or if it took a different form.

That attachment is powerful, and, oh, Dr. Freud, it is alive and well: When my daughter says to her father, "Oh, Daddy, I like your tie," she seems to imply by tone and manner that he nurtured the worms, harvested the silk, designed the pattern, sewed in the lining, and invented the four-in-hand knot, all before breakfast.

My relationship with my father was more man-to-man. He required of a fully developed human being that she have exhaustively studied both Max Shulman and Machiavelli, Django Reinhardt and Louis Armstrong, that she never, ever, call N'Orlins New Or-leeens or Philadelphia Philly. His motto was "winners need not explain." He treated Bs as if they were Fs. He was fast and funny; if you couldn't keep up, you got left.

I kept up.

I was lucky in many ways. I've heard about the men who treat the birth of a girl child as something only slightly better than a death in the family. I've read about Elizabeth Barrett and the poor Brontës. If you look in the index of *Bartlett's Familiar Quotations* for the word "father," there are two full columns of entries. But a large number of those are references to God.

My father exercised only the tyranny of his expectations, but it was tyranny enough. And then, not so many years ago, I realized that, like a heart transplant after the rejection phase, his expectations for me had become my own. And I stopped valuing myself by how my father valued me. I know from literature and life that that is perhaps the greatest passage that human beings ever make.

In her novel *The Lost Father*, Mona Simpson writes of one woman's odyssey to find the parent who had abandoned her. "I decided if I ever saw him again he would not be my father, but just a man," she says. But of course it is not really her father she is looking for at all, but herself. "I'm still looking, just not there," she concludes after the father has been found, and found wanting.

"There's an axiom in Zen Buddhism that goes something like

this," the novelist Mark Leyner said when his father was being honored at a testimonial dinner. "Before you study Zen, a mountain is just a mountain; while you study Zen, a mountain is more than a mountain; when you've finished studying Zen, a mountain is just a mountain."

I confess that this is the first Zen wisdom that has ever seized my fancy instantly. My father is just a mountain to me now, a man and not a mirror. This enables me to love him as I never could when I saw only my own splayed reflection in the lenses of his glasses. His expectations were hard on me, but they took me places I would never have gone otherwise. A curse, a blessing, all in one. We might as well have a universal support group: Adult Children of Parents.

I have never understood those people who believe it is possible to cut the ties that bind without taking a big chunk out of yourself. My first word was Bob, which is my father's name. Perhaps it was when I had children myself that I lost the habit, carried well into adulthood, of seeing him through a child's eyes.

I was less the daughter of the groom at his wedding than I was the mother of the flower girl, worried more about whether she would lift her flowered skirts over her head during the ceremony than how I felt about yet another woman in my father's life. My father says my daughter is much like me when small. And my daughter loves her daddy so. And so it goes, has always gone, will always go.

Fall from the Nest

JUNE 1994

THE CARDINALS WERE in the sunroom downstairs, battling the deceptive transparency of the windows. They were a matched pair, his and hers, with the air of belonging together and being there for a purpose. The purpose was on the floor, a chick with the rheumy rolling eye and bony neck of an old man. The door had been left open for the dog, and the baby had come in, its parents close behind. I took the chick back outside and opened the windows for its parents, who fluttered overhead, making the monosyllabic monotonous note of the cardinal, tinged now with a palpable air of distress.

The chick had legs like *L*s, pale and sinewy, and wings that seemed twice the size necessary to lift its body. It rose and fell, rose and fell again. All day long its mother, soft brown with a bright beak, and its father, a flamboyant flag of crimson against the leaves, followed it around the yard, making frantic one-note suggestions.

Once I tried to place it in the thick branches of the forsythia bush close to its nest, its heart beating against my palm like my own pulse. It screamed in distress, and the parents flew close to my head. All day I watched from the window for stray cats. At nightfall the birds were suddenly silent.

Why worry? Baby birds are cheap as feathers; nature is hard and accidents happen. Once when I was a child we found a nest of bunnies beneath the stiffening corpse of their mother. We fed them with eyedroppers, cosseted them in a basket, kept them by the radiator, and peeked at them at night, their eyes like bits of onyx catching any light in the darkness. One by one they died. Even my mother wept.

Now I know that much of parenthood is watching and waiting for the chick to fall into harm's way, watching and waiting for the cats and the cold nights. The joyous enterprise has an undercurrent of terror. Part of the reason for the palpable happiness of this commencement season is the great relief of knowing that some danger point is past, whether in high school in South Central L.A. or college in Cambridge. Some times and some places are far more perilous than others. But having children is always a perilous undertaking.

It's the randomness of it that is so awful as we clutch close our little constructions of family and home and school, an artful web of twigs. Children step in front of cars and fall into pools; teenagers take the wrong drugs, drive too fast, dip too deep into some well of despair. Some get stuck in the tar of the bad spots, and some do not. Some grow up strong with bad upbringings, and some falter with good ones.

In front of me, stuck in the corner of a picture frame, is a black-and-white photograph. In the doorway of a dining room with dark patterned wallpaper is a young woman holding an infant. Behind her, the table is set for dinner. In the mirror over the sideboard is reflected a man in the living room beyond, a young man in khakis and a white shirt. The man is the woman's husband, the baby's father. The baby is me.

In profile, her head dipped down over the infant's, my mother looks as if she is speaking in the picture, and sometimes I think she is telling me a secret, and that if only I can read her lips I will know how she intends to keep me safe. But the secret is that there is no secret. There is no formula, much as I once looked for one in the pages of Spock and Penelope Leach, believing that child-rearing was algebra and that if I studied hard enough I would succeed.

In a second photograph my mother and father are standing on the lawn. Both of them are handsomely dressed and he is holding another baby, dressed in christening robes. You can see the way the picture was meant to look by the way he is posed for the camera. But at the moment the shutter clicked my mother lunged forward, her hand open and outstretched, to grab the toddler running out of the frame, a blur of bonnet and matching coat, the baby of the first photograph, ambulatory and a little less safe than before. That lunge is the lesson.

I still see the two adult cardinals from the window, and their cries have gone back to the empty one-note I've learned to recognize as peculiar to the breed. Maybe the chick learned to fly. Or maybe sometime I will find its tiny toothpick bones amid the ivy. And I will never know why or how it fell, what would have been required for it to escape disaster. I think of this often, though not really about the birds.

The *C* Word
in the Hallways

NOVEMBER 1999

THE SADDEST PHRASE I'VE READ in a long time is this one: psychological autopsy. That's what the doctors call it when a kid kills himself, and they go back over the plowed ground of his short life, and discover all the hidden markers that led to the rope, the blade, the gun.

There's a plague on all our houses, and since it doesn't announce itself with lumps or spots or protest marches, it has gone unremarked in the quiet suburbs and busy cities where it has been laying waste. The number of suicides and homicides committed by teenagers, most often young men, has exploded in the last three decades, until it has become routine to have black-bordered photographs in yearbooks and murder suspects with acne problems. And everyone searches for reasons, and scapegoats, and solutions, most often punitive. Yet one solution continues to elude us, and that is ending the ignorance about mental health, and moving it from the margins of care and into the mainstream where it belongs. As surely as any vaccine, this would save lives.

So many have already been lost. This month Kip Kinkel was sentenced to life in prison in Oregon for the murders of his parents and a shooting rampage at his high school that killed two students. A psychiatrist who specializes in the care of adolescents testified that Kinkel, now seventeen, had been hearing voices since he was twelve. Sam Manzie is also seventeen. He is serving a seventy-year sentence for luring an eleven-year-old boy named Eddie Werner into his New Jersey home and strangling him with the cord to an alarm clock because his Sega Genesis was out of reach. Manzie had his first psychological evaluation in the first grade.

Excuses, excuses. That's what so many think of the underlying pathology in such hideous crimes. In the 1956 movie *The Bad Seed,* little Patty McCormack played what was then called a "homicidal maniac" and the film censors demanded a ludicrous mock curtain call in which the child actress was taken over the knee of her screen father and spanked. There are still some representatives of the "good spanking" school out there, although today the spanking may wind up being life in prison. And there's still plenty of that useless adult "what in the world does a sixteen-year-old have to be depressed about" mind-set to keep depressed sixteen-year-olds from getting help.

It's true that both the Kinkel and the Manzie boys had already been introduced to the mental health system before their crimes. Concerned by her son's fascination with weapons, Faith Kinkel took him for nine sessions with a psychologist in the year before the shootings. Because of his rages and his continuing relationship with a pedophile, Sam's parents had tried to have him admitted to a residential facility just days before their son invited Eddie in.

But they were threading their way through a mental health system that is marginalized by shame, ignorance, custom, the courts, even by business practice. Kip Kinkel's father made no secret of his disapproval of therapy. During its course he bought his son the Glock that Kip would later use on his killing spree, which speaks sad volumes about our peculiar standards of masculinity. Sam's father, on the other hand, spent days trying to figure out how much of the cost of a home for troubled kids his insurance would cover. In the meantime, a psychiatrist who examined his son for less time than it takes to eat a Happy Meal concluded that he was no danger to himself or others, and a judge lectured Sam from the bench: "You know the difference between right and wrong, don't you?"

The federal Center for Mental Health Services estimates that at least six million children in this country have some serious emotional disturbance and, for some of them, right and wrong take second seat to the voices in their heads. Fifty years ago their parents might have surrendered them to life in an institution, or a doctor flying blind with an ice pick might have performed a lobotomy, leaving them to loll away their days. Now lots of them wind up in jail. Warm fuzzies aside, consider this from a utilitarian point of view: Psychological intervention is cheaper than incarceration.

The most optimistic estimate is that two thirds of these emotionally disturbed children are not getting any treatment. Imagine how we would respond if two thirds of America's babies were not being immunized. Many health insurance plans do not provide coverage for necessary treatment, or financially penalize those who need a psychiatrist instead of an oncologist. Teachers are not trained to recognize mental illness, and some dismiss it, "Bad Seed" fashion, as bad behavior. Parents are afraid, and

ashamed, creating a home environment, and a national atmosphere, too, that tells teenagers their demons are a disgrace.

And then there are the teenagers themselves, slouching
toward adulthood in a world that loves conformity. Add to the
horror of creeping depression or delusions that of peer derision,
the sound of the *C* word in the hallways: crazy, man, he's crazy,
haven't you seen him, didn't you hear? Boys, especially, still suspect that talk therapy, or even heartfelt talk, is somehow sissi-
fied, weak. Sometimes even their own fathers think so, at least
until they have to identify the body.

Another sad little phrase is "If only," and there are always
plenty of them littering the valleys of tragedy. If only there had
been long-term intervention and medication, Kip Kinkel might
be out of jail, off the taxpayers' tab, and perhaps leading a pro-
ductive life. If only Sam Manzie had been treated aggressively
earlier, new psychotropic drugs might have slowed or stilled his
downward slide. And if only those things had happened, Faith
Kinkel, William Kinkel, Mikael Nickolauson, Ben Walker, and
Eddie Werner might all be alive today. Mental health care is
health care, too, and mental illness is an illness, not a character
flaw. Insurance providers should act like it. Hospitals and schools
should act like it. Above all, we parents should act like it. Then
maybe the kids will believe it.

School's Out
for Summer

JUNE 2001

WHEN THE AD COUNCIL CONVENED focus groups not long ago to help prepare a series of public service announcements on child hunger, there was a fairly unanimous response from the participants about the subject. Not here. Not in America. If there was, we would know about it. We would read about it in the paper, we would see it on the news. And of course we would stop it. In America.

Is it any wonder that the slogan the advertising people came up with was "The Sooner You Believe It, the Sooner We Can End It"?

It's the beginning of summer in America's cement cities, in the deep hidden valleys of the country and the loop-de-loop side-walkless streets of the suburbs. For many adults who are really closet kids, this means that their blood hums with a hint of freedom, the old beloved promise of long aimless days of dirt and sweat and sunshine, T-shirts stained with Kool-Aid and flip-flops gray with street grit or backyard dust.

But that sort of summer has given way to something more difficult, even darker, that makes you wonder whether year-round school is not a notion whose time has come. With so many households in which both parents are working, summer is often a scramble of scheduling: day camps, school programs, the Y, the community center. Some parents who can't afford or find those kinds of services park their vacationing children in front of the television, lock the door, and go to work hoping for the best, calling home on the hour. Some kids just wander in a wilder world than the one that existed when their parents had summers free.

And some kids don't get enough to eat, no matter what people want to tell themselves. Do the math: During the rest of the year fifteen million students get free or cut-rate lunches at school, and many of them get breakfast, too. But only three million children are getting lunches through the federal summer lunch program. And hunger in the United States, particularly since the institution of so-called welfare reform, is epidemic. The numbers are astonishing in the land of the all-you-can-eat buffet. The Agriculture Department estimated in 1999 that twelve million children were hungry or at risk of going hungry. A group of big-city mayors released a study showing that in 2000, requests for food assistance from families increased almost 20 percent, more than at any time in the last decade. And last Thanksgiving a food bank in Connecticut gave away four thousand more turkeys than the year before—and still ran out of birds.

But while the Christmas holidays make for heartrending copy, summer is really ground zero in the battle to keep kids fed. The school lunch program, begun in the 1970s as a result of bipartisan federal legislation, has been by most measures an enormous success. For lots of poor families it's become a way to count on getting at least one decent meal into their children, and when it disappears it's catastrophic. Those who work at America's Second Harvest, the biggest nonprofit supply source for food banks, talk of parents who go hungry themselves so their kids can eat, who put off paying utility and phone bills, who insist their children attend remedial summer school programs simply so they can get a meal. The parents themselves are loath to talk: Of all the humiliations attached to being poor in a prosperous nation, not being able to feed your kids is at the top of the list.

In most cases these are not parents who are homeless or out of work. The people who run food banks report that most of their clients are minimum-wage workers who can't afford enough to eat on their salaries. "Families are struggling in a way they haven't done for a long time," says Brian Loring, the executive director of Neighborhood Centers of Johnson County, Iowa, which provides lunches to more than two hundred kids at five locations during the summer months. For a significant number of Americans, the cost of an additional meal for two school-age children for the eight weeks of summer vacation seems like a small fortune. Some don't want or seek government help because of the perceived stigma; some are denied food stamps because of new welfare policies. Others don't know they're eligible, and none could be blamed if they despaired of the exercise. The average length of a food stamp application is twelve often impenetrable pages; a permit to sell weapons is just two.

The success of the school lunch program has been, of course, that the food goes where the children are. That's the key to success for summer programs, too. Washington, D.C., has done better than any other city in the country in feeding hungry kids, sending fire trucks into housing projects to distribute leaflets about lunch locations, running a referral hotline and radio announcements. One food bank in Nevada decided to send trucks to the parks for tailgate lunches. "That's where the kids are," its director told the people at Second Harvest.

We Americans like need that takes place far from home, so we can feel simultaneously self-congratulatory and safe from the possibility that hard times could be lurking around the corner. Maybe that's why our mothers told us to think of the children in Africa when we wouldn't clean our plates. I stopped believing in that when I found myself in a bodega with a distraught woman after New York City had declared a snow day; she had three kids who ate breakfast and lunch at school, her food stamps had been held up because of some bureaucratic snafu, and she was considering whether to pilfer food from the senior center where she worked as an aide. Surely there should be ways for a civilized society to see that such a thing would never happen, from providing a simpler application for food stamps to setting a decent minimum wage. But wishing don't make it so, as they say in policy meetings, and proposals aren't peanut butter and jelly. Find a food bank and then go grocery shopping by proxy. Somewhere nearby there is a mother who covets a couple of boxes of spaghetti, and you could make her dream come true. That's right. In America.

A New Roof
on an Old House

JUNE 2000

A SLATE ROOF IS A HUMBLING THING. The one we're putting on the old farmhouse is Pennsylvania blue-black, and it's meant to last at least a hundred years. Jeff the roof guy showed us the copper nails he's using to hang it; they're supposed to last just as long. So will the massive beams upon which the slates rest. "Solid as a cannonball," Jeff says. Looking up at the roof taking shape slate by enduring slate, it is difficult not to think about the fact that by the time it needs to be replaced, we will be long gone.

In this fast-food, face-lift, no-fault-divorce world of ours, the slate roof feels like the closest we will come to eternity. It, and the three children for whom it is really being laid down.

Another Mother's Day has come and gone as the roofers work away in the pale May sun and the gray May rain. It is a silly holiday, and not for all the reasons people mention most, not because it was socially engineered to benefit card shops, florists, and those who slake the guilt of neglect with once-a-year homage. It is silly because something as fleeting and finite as twenty-four hours is the antithesis of what it means to mother a child. That is the work of the ages.

This is not only because the routine is relentless, the day-in/day-outness of hastily eaten meals, homework help, and heart-to-hearts, things that must be done and done and then done again. It is that if we stop to think about what we do, really do, we are building for the centuries. We are building character, and tradition, and values, which meander like a river into the distance and out of our sight, but on and on and on.

If any of us engaged in the work of mothering thought much about it as the task of fashioning the fine points of civilization, we would be frozen into immobility by the enormity of the task. It is like writing a novel: If you consider it the creation of a four-hundred-page manuscript, the weight of the rock and the pitch of the hill sometimes seem beyond ken and beyond effort. But if you think of your work as writing sentences—well, a sentence is a manageable thing.

And so is one hour of miniature golf, one tête-à-tête under the covers, one car ride with bickering in the backseat, one kiss, one lecture, one Sunday morning in church. One slate laid upon another, and another, and in the end, if you have done the job with care and diligence, you have built a person, reasonably resistant to the rain. More than that, you have helped build the future of her spouse, his children, even their children's children, for good or for ill. *Joie de vivre*, bitterness, consideration, carelessness: They are as communicable as chicken pox; exposure can lead to infection. People who hit their children often have children who hit their children. Simple and precise as arithmetic, that. "Careful the things you say, children will listen," sings the mother witch in Stephen Sondheim's *Into the Woods*. And listen and listen and listen, until they've heard, and learned.

There is a great variety of opinion about mothering because

there is great variety in the thing itself. In *Sons and Lovers,* D. H. Lawrence renders Mother an emotional cannibal, trying to consume her children. Mrs. Bennet of *Pride and Prejudice* is a foolish auctioneer, seeking the highest bidder for her girls. Mrs. Portnoy hectors, hilariously. It is no coincidence that these are all, in some way, richly unsatisfactory, even terrifying mothers (and that their creators were not mothers themselves). The power of the role creates a powerful will to dismiss, ridicule, demonize, and so break free.

Fat chance, Freudians. Whether querulous or imperious, attentive or overbearing, warm or waspish, surcease or succubus, she is as central as the sun. During our lifetime motherhood has been trashed as a dead-end no-pay career and elevated as a sacred and essential calling. It is neither. It is a way of life, chosen in great ignorance, and the bedrock of much of what we are, and will become.

The flowers sent under the auspices of that gauzy pink second Sunday in May have browned now, and the cards that stood in repose on the mantel have been consigned, with their elder sisters, to the bottom of the jewelry box or the bureau drawer. All this has as much to do with mothering as a blue spruce lopped off at the trunk and strung with glass has to do with the message of Christianity. Mothering consists largely of transcendent scut work, which seems contradictory, which is exactly right. How can you love so much someone who drives you so crazy and makes such constant demands? How can you devote yourself to a vocation in which you are certain to be made peripheral, if not redundant? How can we joyfully embrace the notion that we have ceased to be the center of our own universe?

There is the roof, growing larger and stronger, one small piece after another making a great whole, until it can withstand winds and heat and blizzards and downpours. It is a utilitarian thing, and a majestic one, too. There are ghosts beneath its eaves, ghosts yet to be born, the ghosts of my children's grown children, saying, "Our grandparents put that roof on the house in the year 2000." And if I could speak through the opaque curtain of time I would say, "We did it to keep you safe and warm, so that you could do your best by you and yours, just as we have tried to do." Perhaps I would be talking to myself, because the house had been sold, the roof given over to shelter other people's children. That's all right, too. It's the thought that counts, and the metaphor. In the sharply angled gray lines against the lambent sky I can read reports of my own inevitable passing. But I see my immortality, too, the part of me that will live forever.

An Apology
to the Graduates

MAY 2004

MEMBERS OF THE CLASS OF 2004: I'M SO SORRY. I look at all
of you and realize that, for many, life has been a relentless treadmill since you entered preschool at the age of two. Sometimes, as
though I am narrating a fairy story, I tell my children of a time
when the SAT was taken only once and a tutor was a character in
an English novel, when I could manage to pay my own college
tuition with summer wages and find both a good job and a decent
apartment when I graduated.

Now cottage industries have grown up around the impossibility of any of that: specialized learning centers to supplement
schools, special loan programs at usurious rates to supplement college grants, companies that will throw up instant walls
to turn a one-bedroom apartment into a place where three people
can coexist.

There's an honorable tradition of starving students; it's just
that, between the outsourcing of jobs and a boom market in real

estate, your generation envisions becoming starving adults. Caught in our peculiar modern nexus of prosperity and insolvency, easy credit, and epidemic bankruptcy, you also get toxic messages from the culture about what achievement means. It is no longer enough to make it; you must make it *big*. Television has turned everything into a contest, from courtship to adoption. In a voyeuristic world, fame becomes a ubiquitous career goal.

You all will live longer than any generation in history, yet you were kicked into high gear earlier as well. How exhausted you must be. Your college applications look like the résumés for mid-level executives. We boomer moms and dads had high expectations, ratcheted up by what the more honest of us must admit was something akin to competitive parenting. Soccer leagues. Language programs. Even summer camps that concentrate on college prep instead of sailing.

Your grandparents surely think that it was more stressful to join the service after Pearl Harbor, and at some level they're right. But the mission was clear then, the goal straightforward and honorable, the endgame a good life and a healthy family. What is it now? Public buildings were once named after war heroes, philanthropists, and presidents, but in New Jersey one school has managed to keep its gym spiffy by taking money from the local supermarket and putting up a big sign: THE SHOPRITE OF BROOKLAWN CENTER. Cash is the point. Who wants to be a millionaire? Everyone. Although a million doesn't buy what it once did. Just look at the bottom line on your college loans.

Who can blame you if you were not all creating Campus Coalitions for Peace or People for the Ethical Treatment of People? It was not marches or leafleting that drove the political process as you grew up, but soft money and PACs. It now costs so much to run a race for public office that the contribution of any individual may seem puny and irrelevant. Your commencements will take place in the shadow of the revelation that some American troops, styled as heroic liberators, were instead sadistic humiliators in the prisons of Iraq. You new women have a new anti–role model, the G.I. Jane photographed pointing at the genitals of a naked Iraqi and smirking.

One professor at the University of Maryland who was at the college during the sixties and remembers thousands gathering to protest the Vietnam War told the Baltimore *Sun* the activist days are gone forever: "They're interested in their grades and then getting a good job when they get out." It's easy to translate this transformation into vacuous careerism, but it's something more complex than that. Here is a remarkably incisive summation from Lillian Mongeau, who will graduate from Barnard College later this month:

"When telling my family history I proudly tell how each generation sacrificed so that the next could achieve more—more education, more money, more prestige. But how can I achieve more than my parents? They are living the American dream. Now if I don't achieve as much as they did I will have failed, but to achieve more than they did is virtually impossible. To this is the added pressure that there is no excuse for failure. I have had the best of everything. . . . If I mess up it will be entirely my fault.

"I feel that I just need some time," she adds. "I just want everything to stop moving for a while so that I can think."

To the members of the class of 2004: Putting a stop to this treadmill is like disarmament. Who dares to go first? A generation ago your parents, as a group, were known for wanting to give peace a chance in the world. Somehow we have raised a group that wants only a little peace in their own frantic lives. But peace is not what you see in the immediate future, for the world, for this nation or for yourselves. Instead, what stretches before you looks like a version of *Survivor* in street clothes. Find the job. Find the mate. Scale the ladder. Have the baby. Make the deal. Make the birthday cake. The gym, the Gap, the lover, the decor, the cuisine. Who will win the contest? Perhaps it will be those of you brave enough to stop moving.

Flown Away, Left Behind

JANUARY 2004

I WAS SOMETHING OF AN ACCIDENTAL MOTHER. I don't mean that in the old traditional whoops! way; it's just that while I barreled through my twenties convinced that having a baby would be like carrying a really large and inconvenient tote bag that I could never put down, I awoke one day at thirty and, in what now seems an astonishingly glib leap of faith, decided I wanted that tote bag in the very worst way. It was as though my ovaries had taken possession of my brain. Less than a year later an infant had taken possession of everything else. My brain no longer worked terribly well, especially when I added to that baby another baby less than two years later, and a third fairly soon after that.

That was twenty years ago. You do the math. The first one went to China to polish his Mandarin. The second left for college in the fall. I still have a chick in the nest, and what a chick she is, but increasingly it feels like an aerie too large for its occupants. Recently I told her we were going to be doing something we had always done as a family. "We don't have that family any-more," she said. (Here I pause to remove the shiv from between my ribs, breathe deeply, and smile.)

Tell me at your peril that the flight of my kids into successful adulthood is hugely liberating, that I will not believe how many hours are in the day, that my husband and I can see the world, that I can throw myself into my job. My world is in this house, and I already had a great job into which I'd thrown myself for two decades. No, not the writing job—the motherhood job. I was good at it, if I do say so myself, and because I was, I've now been demoted to part-time work. Soon I will attain emerita status. This stinks.

I wonder if this has a particular edge for the women of my generation, who found themselves pursuing mothering in a new sort of way. We professionalized it, and in doing so made our-selves a tiny bit ridiculous and more than a little crazy. Women who left their children in the care of others to work for pay often wound up, by necessity and habit, scheduling their mother life as they did their working one. (See us logging teacher conferences into our PDAs in the parking lot of the preschool.) Women who eschewed the job market despite the gains of women within it sometimes wound up making motherhood into a surrogate work world, full of school meetings and endless athletic teams. (See us chairing bake sales even though it would be cheaper to write a check than to make brownies.) For both groups, the unexamined child was not worth having: from late crawling to bad hand-writing to mediocre SATs, all was grist for the worry mill. Mother-hood changed from a role into a calling. Our poor kids.

The end result is that the empty nest is emptier than ever before; after all, at its center was a role, a vocation, a nameless something so enormous that a good deal had to be sacrificed for it, whether sleep or self or money or ambition or peace of mind.

Those sacrifices—or accommodations, for those of us waxing poetic about their end—became the warp and woof of our lives; first we got used to them and then before we knew it they had become obsolete. Those of you waiting for your babies to sleep through the night will be amazed how quickly they come to sleep through the afternoon after a night out.

For years I wrote only between the hours of nine and three, when the children were at school. (God forbid they should actually see me work.) Now that two of the children live at school and one has play rehearsal, basketball games, and random hanging-out when school is done, I still write only between the hours of nine and three. It has become my routine; I did not choose to change it. In the kitchen is a magnet that says MOM IS NOT MY REAL NAME. See our heads snap up in the supermarket when someone yells the word, as surely as our milk once let down when we heard a baby, any baby, cry.

Much has been written about the pernicious nature of having it all, the perfection syndrome required of women who must play so many roles in the lives of others, jamming loving obligations into days that feel too short, discussing endlessly how to balance work and home. But many of us eventually ratcheted up our metabolisms accordingly. First overfull was a cross, then a challenge, eventually a commonplace. Anything less is empty.

It's not simply the loss of these particular people, living here day in, day out, the bickering, the inside jokes, the cereal bowls in the sink, and the towels in the hamper—all right, on the floor. It's who I was with them: the general to their battalion, the president to their cabinet. The Harpo to their Groucho, Zeppo, and Chico. Sometimes I go into their rooms and just stand, touching their books, looking out their windows. "The shrine," the youngest says derisively, although she misses the other two as much as I do. But she has her own plans, has one eye now on the glitter past the window glass. At the end of the month she heads Down Under on a six-week school exchange, leaving the bulletin board, the photograph albums, and the wallpaper with butterflies on it behind. And me, of course. Three rooms empty, full of the ghosts of my very best self. Mom is my real name. It is, it is.

2 Mind

THE TWO ESSAYS THAT FEEL MOST DATED in my last collection of columns are, ironically, the two that I shoehorned into the manuscript at the last possible moment because of time constraints. Both of them were written with a burst of happiness and hope.

One feels as though it happened in another time and place simply because of the passage of the years. It is about my daughter's second birthday. The fireplug toddler to whom it pays tribute is today a young woman of beauty and poise. Still, I feel a sense of satisfaction because I somehow nailed her essential nature long ago in a single sentence: "If personalities had colors, hers would be red." This is probably even truer today than it was then. Crimson, scarlet, fuchsia, magenta: She is a blaze of a human being.

The second essay is sadder for me to read. My powers of prediction were as wrong as my flagrant idealism. It is entitled "A Place Called Hope," and it is about how voting for Bill Clinton lifted my spirits in a way no political act of my adult life had done before.

Sigh.

I missed most of the worst of the Clinton years, not as a citizen, certainly, but as a columnist. During the Lewinsky scandal I was working only in fiction, and never was I happier that it was not necessary for me to consider, to explain, to pass judgment. It was neither a good time to be a liberal nor a Democrat; it was an even less felicitous time to be a pundit. Even for a two-term Democrat, Clinton was loathed by a significant segment of the Republican Party. And because his intellect and political savvy had promised such great things in 1992, his subsequent failures of character, the squandering of a long-awaited opportunity, made many Democrats hate him as well. Hell hath no fury like an idealist disenchanted.

Perhaps the atmosphere surrounding electoral politics and power in the United States would have degenerated even without this catalyst. But the seeds of anomie and cynicism, planted deep in the years of Vietnam and Watergate, bloomed handsomely when faced with late-night TV hosts chortling over the spectacle of a blue dress stained with the president's fluids. The president became the subject of a hundred dirty jokes, and so, by extension, did the political process.

The civic-minded searched for ways to increase voting rates, but they remained deplorably low. The influential media became more TV, less print; the TV media became more cable, less network, and louder, meaner, more shoutfest than talk show. The point of politics had always been at some level to prevail, but the use of that dignified term seemed absurd: The point was to win, to dirty up the other guy until he keeled over and you could pump your fist in the air. Increasingly the body politic seemed to refer, not to the ordinary American citizen, but to a small group of men and women sealed within the bell jar of the capital and the Capitol Building, out of touch not only with what their constituents felt but with what they themselves believed.

The focus group ruled.

Perhaps I am painting the worst possible picture here. Some readers suggested that there was an obvious and deplorable reason for that, as I worked my way unhappily through the early Bush II years, the antiterrorism measures, the Iraq war. It was simply that now I was on the losing side. "If Clinton had done this you'd be dancing in the streets," so many e-mail messages and snail mail letters began on so many different issues.

Those messages, and even the ones of support, were chilling because they revealed the astonishing polarity in American society at the beginning of a new century. Perhaps it was merely that the majority remained silent, in the words of Richard Nixon, the president whose fall began this downward slide. But the response was either damning or applauding, either invective or untrammeled praise. I cherished any communication that agreed in some measure, disagreed in others, then went on to discuss and debate. But such responses were few and far between. Gun control, tax cuts, combat, free speech: The mail felt as though it might burst into flames.

It was also dispiriting to see how certain issues had become fixed in the amber of polar opinions. In all the years I have written about abortion, I have never felt that there has been much movement in the crying need to find some way to talk about the issue reasonably. The same is true of the death penalty, and the letter writers of the National Rifle Association are as certain as ever that any gun law is a bad law. And even though the rights of gay men and lesbians have increased significantly since I first discovered that homophobia remained an acceptable bigotry, there are still plenty of people willing to tell you that "they" are trying to seduce our kids and take over our culture. "They": It's the official pronoun of the new polarity. They are black, Mexican, gay, female, liberal, conservative.

The whole notion of America was supposed to be, to borrow the name of Joy Hakim's wonderful history books, The Story of Us. And politics was meant to serve that. It was the watch works, gears and wheels and cogs that fit together to make the thing run properly. The watch itself was democracy, certain to the minute.

I hope someday to believe that the watch is gold again, its mechanism running properly. It is sad for me, that I have not felt that for so long, that many of my most political columns seem partisan even to myself. I am sad to read that election night column, bursting with the overwrought hopes of a forty-year-old woman. It's not that I mind having written it. I mind the suspicion I'll probably never feel moved to write anything like it again.

A Quilt of a Country

SEPTEMBER 2001

AMERICA IS AN IMPROBABLE IDEA. A mongrel nation built of ever-changing disparate parts, it is held together by a notion, the notion that all men are created equal, though everyone knows that most men consider themselves better than someone. "Of all the nations in the world, the United States was built in nobody's image," the historian Daniel Boorstin wrote. That's because it was built of bits and pieces that seem discordant, like the crazy quilts that have been one of its great folk art forms, velvet and calico and checks and brocades.

Out of many, one. That is the ideal.

The reality is often quite different, a great national striving consisting frequently of failure. Many of the oft-told stories of the most pluralistic nation on earth are stories not of tolerance, but of bigotry. Slavery and sweatshops, the burning of crosses and the ostracism of the other. Children learn in social studies class and in the news of the lynching of blacks, the denial of rights to women, the murders of gay men. It is difficult to know how to persuade them that this amounts to "crown thy good with brotherhood," that amid all the failures is something spectacularly successful. Perhaps they understand it at this moment, when enormous tragedy, as it so often does, demands a time of reflection on enormous blessings.

This is a nation founded on a conundrum, what Mario Cuomo has characterized as "community added to individualism." These two are our defining ideals; they are also in constant conflict. Historians today bemoan the ascendancy of a kind of prideful apartheid in America, saying that the clinging to ethnicity, in background and custom, has undermined the concept of unity. These historians must have forgotten the past, or have gilded it. The New York of my children is no more Balkanized, probably less so, than the Philadelphia of my father, in which Jewish boys would walk several blocks out of their way to avoid the Irish divide of Chester Avenue. (I was the product of a mixed marriage, across barely bridgeable lines: an Italian girl, an Irish boy. How quaint it seems now, how incendiary then.) The Brooklyn of Francie Nolan's famous tree, the Newark of which Portnoy complained, even the uninflected WASP suburbs of Cheever's characters: They are ghettos, pure and simple. Do the Cambodians and the Mexicans in California coexist less easily today than did the Irish and Italians of Massachusetts a century ago? You know the answer.

What is the point of this splintered whole? What is the point of a nation in which Arab cabbies chauffeur Jewish passengers through the streets of New York—and in which Jewish cabbies chauffeur Arab passengers, too, and yet speak in theory of hatred, one for the other? What is the point of a nation in which one part seems to be always on the verge of fisticuffs with another, blacks and whites, gays and straights, left and right, Pole and Chinese and Puerto Rican and Slovenian? Other countries with such divisions have in fact divided into new nations with new names, but not this one, impossibly interwoven even in its hostilities.

Once these disparate parts were held together by a common enemy, by the fault lines of world wars and the electrified fence of communism. With the end of the cold war, there was the creeping concern that without a focus for hatred and distrust, a sense of national identity would evaporate, that the left side of the hyphen— African-American, Mexican-American, Irish-American—would overwhelm the right. And slow-growing domestic traumas like economic unrest and increasing crime seemed more likely to emphasize division than community. Today the citizens of the United States have come together once more because of armed conflict and enemy attack. Terrorism has led to devastation—and unity.

Yet even in 1994, the overwhelming majority of those surveyed by the National Opinion Research Center agreed with this statement: "The U.S. is a unique country that stands for something special in the world." One of the things that it stands for is this vexing notion that a great nation can consist entirely of refugees from other nations, that people of different, even warring religions and cultures can live, if not side by side, then on either side of the country's Chester Avenues. Faced with this diversity there is little point in trying to isolate anything remotely resembling a national character, but there are two strains of behavior that, however tenuously, abet the concept of unity.

There is that Calvinist undercurrent in the American psyche that loves the difficult, the demanding, that sees mastering the impossible, whether it be prairie or subway, as a test of character, and so glories in the struggle of this fractured coalescing. And there is a grudging fairness among the citizens of the United States that eventually leads most to admit that, no matter what the English-only advocates try to suggest, the new immigrants are not so different from our own parents or grandparents. Leonel Castillo, former director of the Immigration and Naturalization Service and himself the grandson of Mexican immigrants, once told the writer Studs Terkel proudly, "The old neighborhood Ma-Pa stores are still around. They are not Italian or Jewish or Eastern European any more. Ma and Pa are now Korean, Vietnamese, Iraqi, Jordanian, Latin American. They live in the store. They work seven days a week. Their kids are doing well in school. They're making it. Sound familiar?"

Tolerance is the word used most often when this kind of coexistence succeeds, but tolerance is a vanilla pudding word, standing for little more than the allowance of letting others live unremarked and unmolested. Pride seems excessive, given the American willingness to endlessly complain about them, them being whoever is new, different, unknown, or currently under suspicion. But patriotism is partly taking pride in this unlikely ability to throw all of us together in a country that across its length and breadth is as different as a dozen countries, and still be able to call it by one name. When photographs of the faces of all of those who died in the World Trade Center destruction are assembled in one place, it will be possible to trace in the skin color, the shape of the eyes and the noses, the texture of the hair, a map of the world. These are the representatives of a mongrel nation that somehow, at times like this, has one spirit. Like many improbable ideas, when it actually works, it's a wonder.

Staring Across a
Great Divide

JULY 2002

IN THE 1970S THE PRESIDENT OF HAVERFORD COLLEGE became a totem for those who believed there was a schism between one America and another. John Coleman was a labor economist who took a sabbatical, not just to write a book but to live a life, or several of them. He dug ditches and picked up garbage, worked on a drilling rig and mined marble. When he later wound up in New York City running a foundation, he joined the auxiliary police force, worked as an emergency medical technician, and one winter lived on the streets for ten days to imagine, albeit briefly, the lives of the homeless.

The Coleman experiment, in which one man tried, in his own words, "to walk in other people's shoes," resonates as the administration considers welfare reform. Emboldened by the success of the 1996 measure, which led to a sharp decline in the welfare rolls, Washington politicians want to act again, forcing states to further decrease the number of those entitled to benefits. They are emboldened, too, by the fact that the most nightmarish scenarios conjured up by opponents of the original bill did not materialize, or at least did not come to light: legions of hungry children, thousands of homeless families.

But it would be a mistake to discount the distrust and fear behind those dire predictions because they are one leading edge of a sentiment that now runs as bone deep in America as patriotism. It is the sense that there is a pernicious cognitive dissonance between those who run things and those who merely live with the results. That loud "crack!" we've been hearing for months is a great rift splitting ever wider, between the bloated executive class and the shareholders of corporations, between the hierarchy of the Catholic church and the appalled faithful, between the men in suits responsible for national intelligence and the citizens who believed heretofore that those men had a clue.

In the case of welfare reform, the chasm between political leaders and assistance recipients seems nearly unbridgeable. Has any member of Congress ever tried to live for a month on a welfare check? For that matter, have any of them ever tried to live on the check that a welfare recipient would receive if she were lucky enough to find a job? The minimum wage hasn't been raised in six years; it's still $5.15 an hour, teenage babysitting pay. What about trying the poverty line, which is where more than one in ten American families have taken up residence? That's an annual income below $17,463 for a family of four. Unfortunately a study by the Economic Policy Institute found that a family earning twice that would still fall below a decent standard of living.

If you actually buy milk and gas, that's not news. But many of the decisions that shape day-to-day life seem to be made by people who float, like enormous unmoored zeppelins, over such minutiae of ordinary existence. So corporate officers, with their enormous compensation packages, are remote from both their workers and their consumers. Whistle-blowers have become the new heroes, leadership without arrogance, a bridge between power and humanity.

It has long been true that the wealthy have governed the lives of the poor; the well-connected the lives of the powerless; men the lives of women; rich whites the lives of poor blacks. This was once considered proper, the God-given right of the prosperous according to the doctrine of economic Darwinism. But progress has taught us that such hierarchical decision-making is often foolish, an outmoded vehicle that resists the important information that ordinary people can provide about everything from the assembly line to the welfare line.

Every time some politician refers to welfare as a "handout," you know he's never spent a moment in those endless lines, done the paperwork, or endured the contempt of the caseworkers, or, for that matter, that he's never talked to those caseworkers, who are routinely cursed out and threatened. Every time a politician lets the alliterative phrase "welfare to work" roll off his tongue, you know he hasn't looked for a job in an economy in which even the educated and the experienced are having a hard time. As Douglas MacKinnon, Bob Dole's press secretary, wrote recently on the op-ed page of *The New York Times,* recounting a childhood on public assistance during which his family was evicted thirty-four times, "For far too many lawmakers, welfare recipients are nothing more than statistics or the subject of abstract policy debates."

It's not that the welfare system doesn't need to be reimagined; it remains, twenty-five years after New York State budget director Peter Goldmark described it thus, "hated by those who administer it, mistrusted by those who pay for it, and held in contempt by those who receive it." But it would be useful if it could be reformed by those who understand it. John Coleman, where are you now that we need you? Where are your heirs, those who know that looking down, from an ivory tower, a corner office, a podium, or a pulpit, often leads to little understanding, less useful change, and a view of nothing more illuminating than polished wingtips?

The Widows
and the Wounded

NOVEMBER 1999

IN THE BEGINNING OF THIS YEAR, a Gallup poll asked Americans about the three most important issues facing the country. As has happened so often in the past, guns were scarcely mentioned. But by the time the same question was asked in May, the halls of Columbine High School had become a shooting gallery, and suddenly the laundry list of national ills had changed dramatically. The availability of guns trumped race relations; school violence was mentioned twice as often as social security. War and peace abroad was barely a blip on the screen compared to gun control at home. And perhaps, in some small way, that poll marked a moment when the American people began to wake up and smell the cordite.

Gun laws are an interesting issue in the never-ending civic debate that is this nation, because there is scarcely any true debate about them at all. Polls have long shown that the majority of the American people—even the majority of gun owners—support government efforts to make sure guns are less dangerous and less often in the hands of the violent, the deranged, and the very young.

Which makes any reasonable person wonder how such public consensus can have spawned such an illusion of strife and so much stillborn legislation. The answer is simple. Many of the elected officials who oppose gun laws aren't true believers. To paraphrase Rhett Butler, the cause they believe in is themselves. The National Rifle Association spends millions of dollars each year on well-connected lobbyists and campaign contributions, to those who support them and, perhaps more important, to the opponents of those who do not.

And the NRA is not spending all that money to buy a nice piece of middle ground. Forty years ago the group targeted an Arkansas state legislator named David Pryor for sponsoring a bill making it illegal to leave a loaded rifle in an unattended unlocked car. (Pryor's measure was, of course, a clear violation of the constitutional right to be unbelievably stupid.) The NRA then dogged Mr. Pryor for decades as he rose to serve in the U.S. Senate. Today one of its targets is a Michigan congressman named Bart Stupak, who had the temerity to suggest that he might vote for childproof locks on guns. The NRA's scorched-earth approach has not changed.

But change has come, slowly, incrementally, elsewhere, and you can count it in either polling percentage points or in the body count. Stockton. Jonesboro. Columbine. The daisy chain of toddlers leaving a Jewish community center in California on an unscheduled field trip to safety when a white supremacist started blasting away in August. A part-time publicist named Donna Thomases saw news footage of those kids, so close in age to her own, and by Labor Day had created something called the Million Mom March. The website has had thousands of hits so far from mothers who want to go to Washington on Mother's Day to demand sensible gun laws. Just the other day Ms. Thomases got an e-mail from a mom in Georgia. "I want to help," wrote Judy Harper, whose thirteen-year-old son Jason died when he accidentally shot himself with a handgun.

The recent history of gun law activism has been defined by that sort of bereavement. Sarah Brady worked for years to pass the most important piece of gun legislation in our lifetime, the Brady bill, after her husband was shot and disabled during the assassination attempt on his boss, Ronald Reagan. Carolyn McCarthy worked to build commonsense consensus on gun laws as a member of Congress after her husband was murdered and her son seriously injured by a gunman on the Long Island Rail Road. "Let me go home," she lamented on the House floor after craven career politics killed a gun measure earlier this year. "I love working with all of you people. I think all of you are great. But somehow we sometimes lose sight of why we are all here."

Mrs. McCarthy, whose wounded son cannot hold his own first-born because he's lost the use of one arm, does not forget why she is in Washington. But she has done more than her share, as has Mrs. Brady. It's time the great complacent majority, the 70 or 80 percent of us who think that guns should be available within reason but regulated within reason, too, begin to do ours. Public policy ought not to be made one bullet wound at a time, and the bereaved should not do all the work for luckier families.

The NRA will argue that there are already enough laws on the books, and that the problem is with enforcement. And these arguments would have more weight had the organization not worked tirelessly to undercut the very agencies that enforce gun control statutes. The NRA will argue that gun laws penalize the law-abiding and leave the criminals free to cause bloodshed. And these arguments would have more weight if more than half of the gun deaths each year were not accidents or suicides, and so many of the measures the NRA has opposed were not so sensible and relatively small. (Mrs. Brady remembers likening gun laws to highway speed limits at a speech in Ohio, and being heckled by gun guys who hated speed limits, too.) Child safety locks. A prohibition on the possession of assault weapons by minors. A ban on the importation of large-capacity ammunition clips. It is preposterous to see the gutting of the Second Amendment in any of these. We register cars in this country, but not guns. And as a result, the United States has the highest rate of gun violence among the world's most prosperous nations. In 1997, an astonishing 86 percent of the gun deaths of children under fifteen in the world took place here.

Perhaps it will take one more school shooting to move the majority of Americans into a position more powerful than that of the NRA. Perhaps it will take one more school shooting to move us from people who support gun control to people who vote it. But as we continue to let the widows and the wounded do the work, be warned. That next school may be the one your children attend; the next accident could be close to home. "This child got into things," Mrs. Harper said of Jason. Don't they all.

Welcome to
Animal House

OCTOBER 2000

THE STUDENT OCCUPATION OF BUILDINGS at Columbia University in 1968 remains the zenith or the nadir of all campus protests, depending on your politics. Richard Nixon (he was on the nadir side) warned in its wake that it was "the first major skirmish in a revolutionary struggle to seize the universities of the country."

If Mr. Nixon were alive today, perhaps he would be surprised to learn that the revolutionary struggle is now in defense of beer, basketball, and assorted bad behavior.

College students have settled in to campuses across America, with their backpacks, their laptops, and their some-assembly-required bookshelves, and as certain as carbohydrates in the food service menu, sooner or later there will be keening about how the poor kids are awash in a welter of political correctness. "Menstruation and Medea: Fear of the Female in the Classics," or "From the Slave Cabins to the Recording Studio: Black in a White Economy"—it's so easy to lampoon the lament that campus life is infused with hyperannuated regard for the sensibilities of minority students and women. There is a sadly out-of-date white Anglo-Saxon term for this point of view. It is balderdash.

The real prevailing ethos on many campuses is quite the opposite. Take the uprisings this semester at Indiana University. These demonstrations were inspired not by the economic disparity between rich and poor or free trade agreements, but by the firing of a man who coaches basketball. Space here is limited, so it is not possible to describe all the boorish behavior for which the Indiana coach, Bobby Knight, has become known over the years. He's thrown furniture, assaulted players, verbally abused both school officials and referees, cursed at opponents, and won a lot of games.

Obviously Mr. Knight's personal style made a huge impact on campus, since students responded to his long-overdue dismissal by setting fires, toppling light poles, and so menacing the president of the university that he and his wife fled their home and moved into a hotel. "History was in the making, and I was not going to miss this for the world, and certainly not for homework," one dopey student, whose parents should stop payment on his tuition check *immediately*, wrote of the riot.

This reaction was not totally unexpected. A professor of English, Murray Sperber, who has been critical of Knight in print and on television, was on leave last year from the university, in part because of letters like the one with the Star of David repeatedly scribbled on it, or the voice-mail message "If you don't shut up, I'll shut you up." In his book *Beer and Circus: How Big-Time College Sports Is Crippling Undergraduate Education,* Professor Sperber says that at schools like Indiana with prominent and successful sports programs, athletics overshadow scholarship, leading to a culture in which students spend more time partying than studying, in which a basketball coach can be infinitely more important than the school's president.

But the Animal House effect in higher education is not confined to big state schools with monster sports teams. MIT, one of the finest science schools in the world, recently agreed to pay almost $5 million to the family of a student who died of acute alcohol poisoning during a fraternity pledge event. Any number of colleges have identified the fraternity culture of long nights and endless kegs as a source of problems ranging from vandalism to date rape, but students respond badly to any attempt to curtail the Greek system. Really badly. When she was president at Denison, Michele Tolela Myers decided that the fraternities at the Ohio school should be nonresidential to cut down on the boozing and bad behavior.

"Frat boys put dead animals outside the front door of our house, someone threw a billiard ball through our living room window," recalled Myers, who is now president of Sarah Lawrence. And it was clear that the students had learned at the knee of like-minded adults. Myers got name-calling hate mail from alums: "the bitch, the Jew, she should go back east where she belongs." So much for PC.

Contrary to all the nattering about political correctness, the social atmosphere on many campuses is macho and exclusionary and determinedly anti-intellectual. It's an atmosphere in which much of the social life revolves around drinking. It's an atmosphere in which date rape is rampant. One study says that six or seven out of every fifty college women have been victims of acquaintance rape within the last year; another says one in four will be sexually assaulted during a college career. It may be provocative to suggest that the new civility codes and sexual assault policies on certain campuses are a product of oversensitivity about issues of race and gender. But it's more accurate to say that they are long-overdue responses to problems of speech and behavior that have been ignored for years because they would cast opprobrium on institutions that prefer applicants see them as their view books do.

The Columbia protests marked the beginning of the end of in loco parentis, the notion that the administration stood in for parents in terms of setting limits and making rules. But Myers's experience indicates that if officials are willing to take a strong stand against individuals and organizations that poison a community—and are willing to put up with a distressing amount of personal abuse and enforce real-world legal statutes—the end result will be salutary. She recalls that Denison had its best applicant pool of her tenure after the fraternity decision because it was no longer seen by parents and college counselors as an unreconstructed party school. "It changed the culture of the campus," she says.

Americans of my parents' generation were horrified by what happened at Columbia in 1968: the files destroyed, the dean held hostage. But if the actions were questionable, the impulse had meaning: opposition to the war in Vietnam, to the university's research contracts with the Pentagon and its plan to co-opt a park in Harlem to build a gym. Three decades later, and we have campus uprisings dedicated to the preservation of a winning season at any cost. Left wing on campus? Don't be fooled. In lots of places, it's not a political stance. It's a position on the hockey team.

The Drug That Pretends It Isn't

APRIL 2000

SPRING BREAK IN JAMAICA, and the patios of the waterfront bars are so packed that it seems the crowds of students must go tumbling into the aquamarine sea, still clutching their glasses. Even at the airport one drunken young man with a peeling nose argues with a flight attendant about whether he can bring his Red Stripe, kept cold in an insulated sleeve, aboard the plane heading home.

The giggle about Jamaica for American visitors has always been the availability of ganja; half the T-shirts in the souvenir shops have slogans about smoking grass. But the students thronging the streets of Montego Bay seem more comfortable with their habitual drug of choice: alcohol.

Whoops! Sorry! Not supposed to call alcohol a drug. Some of the people who lead antidrug organizations don't like it because they fear it dilutes the message about the "real" drugs, heroin, cocaine, and marijuana. Parents are offended by it; as they try to figure out which vodka bottle came from their party and which from their teenager's, they sigh and say, "Well, at least it's not drugs." And naturally the lobbyists for the industry hate it. They're power guys, these guys: The wine guy is George W.'s brother-in-law, the beer guy meets regularly with House majority whip Tom DeLay. When you lump a cocktail in with a joint, it makes them crazy.

And it's true: Booze and beer are not the same as illegal drugs. They're worse. A policy research group called Drug Strategies has produced a report that calls alcohol "America's most pervasive drug problem" and then goes on to document the claim. Alcohol-related deaths outnumber deaths related to drugs four to one. Alcohol is a factor in more than half of all domestic violence and sexual assault cases. Between accidents, health problems, crime, and lost productivity, researchers estimate alcohol abuse costs the economy $167 billion a year. In 1995 four out of every ten people on probation said they were drinking when they committed a violent crime, while only one in ten admitted using illicit drugs. Close your eyes and substitute the word blah-blah for alcohol in any of those sentences, and you'd have to conclude that an all-out war on blah-blah would result.

Yet when members of Congress tried to pass legislation that would make alcohol part of the purview of the nation's drug czar, the measure failed. Mothers Against Drunk Driving faces opposition to both its education programs and its public service ads from principals and parents who think illicit drugs should be given greater priority. The argument is this: Heroin, cocaine, and marijuana are harmful and against the law, but alcohol is used in moderation with no ill effects by many people.

Here's the counterargument: There are an enormous number of people who cannot and will never be able to drink in moderation. And what they leave in their wake is often more difficult to quantify than DWIs or date rapes. In his memoir *A Drinking Life,*

Pete Hamill describes simply and eloquently the binges, the blackouts, the routine: "If I wrote a good column for the newspaper, I'd go to the bar and celebrate; if I wrote a poor column, I would drink away my regret. Then I'd go home, another dinner missed, another chance to play with the children gone, and in the morning, hung over, thick-tongued, and thick-fingered, I'd attempt through my disgust to make amends." Hamill and I used to drink, when we were younger, at a dark place down a short flight of stairs in the Village called the Lion's Head. There were book jackets covering the walls that I used to look at covertly with envy. But then I got older, and when I passed the Head I sometimes thought of how many books had never been written at all because of the drinking.

Everyone has a friend/an uncle/a coworker/a spouse/a neighbor who drinks too much. A recent poll of seven thousand adults found that 82 percent said they'd even be willing to pay more for a drink if the money was used to combat alcohol abuse. New Mexico and Montana already use excise taxes on alcohol to pay for treatment programs. It's probably just coincidence that, as Drug Strategies reports, the average excise tax on beer is nineteen cents a gallon, while in Missouri and Wisconsin, homes to Anheuser-Busch and Miller, respectively, the tax is only six cents.

A wholesale uprising in Washington against Philip Morris, which owns Miller Brewing and was the largest donor of soft money to the Republicans in 1998, or against Seagram's, which did the same for the Democrats in 1996, doesn't seem likely. Homeschooling is in order, a harder sell than even to elected officials, since many parents prefer lessons that do not require self-examination. Talking about underage drinking and peer pressure lets them off the hook by suggesting that it's all about sixteen-year-olds with six-packs. But the peer group is everywhere, from the frogs that croak "Bud" on commercials to those tiresome folks who behave as if wine were as important as books (it's not) to parents who drink to excess and teach an indelible life lesson.

Prohibition was cooked up to try to ameliorate the damage that drinking does to daily life. It didn't work. But there is always self-prohibition. It's not easy, since all the world's a speakeasy. "Not even wine?" Hamill recalls he was asked at dinner parties after he stopped. Of course, children should not drink, and people who sell them alcohol should be prosecuted. Of course, people should not drink and drive, and those who do should be punished. But twenty-one is not a magic number, and the living room is not necessarily a safe place. There is a larger story that needs to be told, loud and clear, in homes and schools and on commercials given as much prominence and paid for in the same way as those that talk about the dangers of smack or crack: that alcohol is a mind-altering, mood-altering drug, and that lots of people should never start to drink at all. "I have no talent for it," Hamill told friends. Just like that.

The Problem
of the Color Line

MARCH 2000

HERE'S A RIDDLE: Why was the internationally known Princeton professor stopped for driving too slowly on a street where the
speed limit was twenty-five miles per hour? How come a Maryland state trooper demanded to search the car of an attorney who
graduated from Harvard? And why were an accomplished actor, a
Columbia administrator, a graduate student, and a merchandiser
for Donna Karan arrested together in New York although none of
them had done anything wrong?

The answer is elementary: All of the men were black. In some
twisted sense, they were the lucky ones. They were only humiliated. Not, like Rodney King, beaten bloody. Not, like Abner
Louima, sodomized with a broken broomstick. Not, like Amadou
Diallo, killed in a gray blizzard of bullets.

The verdict is in. The jury has spoken. The death of Diallo, a
hardworking African immigrant, was adjudged a terrible accident, not murder, not manslaughter. Louima's assailant is in jail.
Two of the officers who beat King went to prison. There have

been commissions, investigations, demonstrations, public reaction, prayer vigils, op-ed pieces, television segments, classroom dialogues. And so Americans richochet from event to event, speaking of reasonable doubt and prosecutorial competence and ignoring the big picture, the real thing, the most important issue in this country that we try not to talk about. That is, race.

"The problem of the twentieth century is the problem of the color line," summed up W.E.B. Du Bois in 1903. How dispiriting to realize it is the problem of the twenty-first century as well. "Our truncated public discussions of race suppress the best of who and what we are as a people because they fail to confront the complexity of the issue in a candid and critical manner," wrote Cornel West, that suspiciously slow-moving Princeton professor, in his aptly titled monograph *Race Matters*. But in truth there are really no public discussions of race. There are discussions of affirmative action, and single parenthood, and, in the wake of human tragedies like the Diallo killing, of police training and procedures. These are discussions designed to cause the least amount of discomfort to the smallest possible number of white people.

Police officers are just us wearing uniforms. The assumptions they make, the prejudices they carry with them, are the assumptions and prejudices of their roots, their neighborhoods, their society. These are not necessarily the excesses of the egregious bigots, but the ways in which race changes everything, often in subtle or unconscious fashion. It is an astonishing dissonance in a nation allegedly based on equality, that there is a group of our citizens who are assumed, simply by virtue of appearance, to be less. Less trustworthy. Less educated or educable. Less moral. What we need to talk about candidly is something more difficult to apprehend than forty-one shots in an apartment house vestibule. It is the unconscious racial shorthand that shapes assumptions so automatic as to be a series of psychological tics: that the black prep school kid must be there on scholarship, that the black woman with a clutch of kids is careless instead of devoted to the vocation of motherhood. Not the shouts of "nigger" but the subconscious conclusions about everything from family background to taste in music based on color alone which blunt the acceptance of individuality and originality that is the glory of being human.

Some of this is easy to see and to deride. A black electrician gets on the train at night and there is the barely perceptible embrace of purses on the laps of women around him. A black attorney stands with upraised hand and watches the cabs whiz by. A mall security guard trails the only black customer through a department store. When police officers looking for drug dealers in New York threw four professional men in jail—including, ironically, the black actor who plays Coalhouse Walker, harassed by bigots in the musical *Ragtime*—they became suspects by virtue of color alone. On the highways being stopped because of race is so common that there's even a clever name for it: DWB, or Driving While Black. Amadou Diallo's mother is asked to accept that the police who shot her son thought his wallet was a gun. I have two teenage sons, and on weekend nights, when they roam the streets of New York City, I never assume that they will be arrested for something they did not do, or shot, or killed. Their wallets will be seen as wallets.

Poll after poll shows a great gap in understanding, between a white America that believes things are ever so much better and a black America that thinks that is delusionary. And that gap mirrors a gap more important than numbers, between what many of us believe we believe, and the subtle assumptions that creep into our consciousness, and which we are often unwilling to admit are there. For a long time we blamed this chasm on black men and women. We who are white expected them to teach us what it was like to be them, to make us comfortable, and we complained when they did not. *"Why Are All the Black Kids Sitting Together in the Cafeteria?"* Beverly Tatum called her book about the black experience. America is a nation riven by geographic apartheid, with precious few truly integrated neighborhoods, particularly in the suburbs. The great divide between black and white yawns wide with the distance of ignorance, and it is reinforced by the silence of shame.

So the sophistry of the margins continues, the discussions of the LAPD or the foster care system or the failure of black leadership. The flagrant bigotries are discussed; the psychology of how we see one another and what that does to us too often is not. The most talkative nation on earth falls silent in the face of the enormity of the failure, of being two nations across a Mason-Dixon Line of incomprehension and subtle assumptions. Oscar Wilde once called homosexuality "the love that dare not speak its name." But we speak its name all the time now. Sex. Religion. Politics. We talk about them all. But what race means, in all its manifestations large and small, is too often a whisper, our great unspoken issue.

A Conspiracy
of Notebooks

FEBRUARY 2002

LINDA LAY SUFFERED FROM BAD TIMING as well as bad judgment. Who thought it would be a good idea for the wife of the former chairman of Enron to poor-mouth before a national TV audience that probably included hundreds who had lost their savings in the company's spectacular crash-and-burn bankruptcy? Who thought it would be a good idea for her to talk about "fighting for liquidity" amid reports of her husband's decision to divest himself of millions of dollars in Enron stock while encouraging employees to hang in there as their retirement plans lost most of their value? In the annals of damaging damage control, Mrs. Lay's performance ranks right up there with Richard Nixon's "I am not a crook."

But the sorriest statement of a sorry performance concerned Cliff Baxter, an Enron executive described by colleagues as a straight arrow, who committed suicide as the disaster developed. "It's a perfect example," Mrs. Lay said, "of how the media can play such havoc and destruction of people's lives." In other words, it wasn't the company; it was the coverage.

That was where the timing came in. As this extraordinary piece of buck-passing was being aired, Daniel Pearl was being held hostage in Pakistan. Pearl, a *Wall Street Journal* reporter photographed in captivity with a gun to his head, was a member of that self-same "media" to which Mrs. Lay was finding it so convenient to shift blame. There was outrage in this country that militants a world away were literally threatening to kill the messenger. But that's something Americans do figuratively all the time.

Only people with the world's most free and open press and the greatest cornucopia of media outlets in the history of the planet could feel so comfortable trashing the entire enterprise. The American people wouldn't know what had happened in the nation's biggest bankruptcy had the press not jumped on the story, which probably was Mrs. Lay's chief complaint. Admittedly, reporters were a little late coming to the debacle; it has been nearly a year since a *Fortune* magazine writer, Bethany McLean, suggested that the Enron emperor had no clothes. Predictably, she was attacked at the time as unethical, biased, and incompetent by the very same executives who are currently under investigation for massive fraud.

In other parts of the world those guys might have avoided such scrutiny. There's Mozambique, where, according to the Committee to Protect Journalists, "truth is not a defense" in cases of defaming the country's president, or the Congo, where "insulting the army" is punishable by death. CPJ reports that thirty-seven journalists were killed last year in the course of their duties, nine of them while covering the war in Afghanistan. The others included a correspondent for a Bengali-language daily beaten and stabbed, apparently because of his reporting on local crime syndicates; a Chinese reporter with his throat cut in what the authorities described as a suicide but his colleagues suspect was reprisal for his stories about corrupt local politicians; and a Filipino radio program director who was gunned down, probably as a response to his commentaries about police involvement in the drug trade.

The lives of reporters in the United States tend to be less dangerous and more humdrum. Misled by Katie Couric's $65 million contract and the opportunities for *Vanity Fair* correspondents to hang with Tom Cruise, readers and viewers probably don't realize that the median salary of a reporter in this country is around $30,000. According to the Bureau of Labor Statistics, reporters and editors in both print and broadcast news are paid on a par with nurses, teachers, and firefighters. Most of them are not swanning around Le Cirque unveiling their face-lifts; instead they're covering planning board meetings and looking over the police blotter, so that when you wake up and say "What were all those sirens last night on Route 209?" you'll know.

Like many people who use the catchall term "the media" to blame bad publicity for bad behavior, Mrs. Lay is trying to suggest a hungry conspiracy of holier-than-thous. And there's no doubt that there's occasionally been a combative edge to the enterprise. Side by side came Vietnam and Watergate; the reporters covering both were characterized as disloyal lefties for writing that the war was a disaster and the White House corrupt. But when the stories were told, the documents released, the tapes transcribed, it turned out that those reporters, like Ms. McLean, had been right. The result was a kind of boy-who-cried-wolf effect: There is nothing like being told over and over again that you are inflating a third-rate burglary and then discovering it indeed is a cancer on the presidency to make you a little deaf to persistent criticism.

Luckily there are few institutions that come under as much scrutiny as newspapers, magazines, and television broadcasts, and not just by those watching and reading. There are media think tanks, journalism school reviews, and national polling, not to mention the eager willingness of one publication to criticize another. Unlike government or business, most newspapers and magazines even run prominent criticisms of their own work in the letters to the editor column. In recent years several dozen newspapers have installed in-house ombudsmen, who cover the paper's policies and shortcomings. If Enron had had someone providing that sort of oversight, maybe it would still be a thriving company instead of a synonym for cooked books.

The press in this country permits a woman to air her contention that her gazillionaire executive husband was asleep at the switch during what may turn out to be one of the greatest fiscal scandals in corporate history, then lets her blame the press itself for the fallout. What a joke. What an institution! Our critics make for great copy, even though their notion of some vast conspiracy of bloodthirsty notebook holders is as improbable as Roswell. Most reporters are like Daniel Pearl, who just went to Pakistan to write some stories. He would follow the facts and file some copy that would allow *Journal* readers, most of whom probably make a lot more money than he did, to understand the complex problems of the region. The irony is that his kidnappers likely thought they were grabbing a man of great status in his own country. As Mrs. Lay's comments suggest and journalists understand, the reality is often quite different.

Happy Leader,
Happy Nation

JANUARY 2001

BENEATH THE MILITARY BLUE TENT that the Big Apple Circus pitches each holiday season in New York City labors a man named Serge Percelly, who juggles tennis rackets. Like other feats that seem both hugely difficult and absolutely pointless—contortionism, for example, or Steven Seagal movies—the first response to this one is "why?" But skepticism withers in the face, not of Mr. Percelly's skill, which is considerable, but of his affect, which is incandescent and irresistible. Two rackets spin, three, four, five, and the curve of the paddle is echoed in the arc of his delighted grin. There is nothing so grand in all the world as watching a person who loves what he does do it.

Which brings us to George W. Bush.

Some transition, huh? Which is probably what the Republicans are saying right about now.

But here's my theory: that the nation is happiest when its leader is obviously happy in his work. Oh, I know happiness has gone out of style, replaced by empowerment and self-esteem. But seeing, in the center ring of the political circus, a person who appears to have a job he loves with all his heart is bracing, even uplifting for the country as a whole, in a fashion sub-rosa, sub-conscious, but substantial. We know this from experience.

In the last twenty-five years the country has had two presidents who adored the job but for quite different reasons. When right-wing operatives torture themselves with how Bill Clinton managed to beat the rap, they might consider the sheer pleasure of observing someone with the glow of knowing he knows everything. The policy wonk's policy wonk, he could rattle off the details of the welfare rolls in Alabama, the acreage in the national forests, the effect of the Asian markets on the Eurodollar. And he could spit it all back in a speech that seemed to be coming straight at you, with a studied sincerity hypnotic as a snake charmer's song. That's one reason why, despite his personal behavior, his approval rating stayed high.

Ronald Reagan loved being president, too. It was the lead role, and the former actor was happy to play it that way, leaving the micromanaging to the cadre of supporting smart guys who stayed at their desks while he took the podium. When, on their anniversary, Reagan sent Nancy a homemade proclamation— "As Pres. Of the U.S., it is my honor & privilege to cite you for service above and beyond the call of duty in that you have made one man (me) the most happy man *in the world* for 29 years"—it was not only the action of a man who was wild about his wife but also wild about his position. The power, the pomp, the incredible, indubitable fact: I rule! Reagan exuded the confidence, not of intellect, but pride of place. That's one reason why, despite his disastrous policies, his popularity was huge.

By contrast, Jimmy Carter, a man of principle and not of politics, made the presidency seem like the Stations of the Cross, his burden to bear. George Bush the elder often had the pinched look of the dyspeptic, perhaps because he thought he was inheriting morning in America and instead wound up with nightfall on Wall Street. Both men were saddled with a sagging economy, unemployment, low consumer confidence. But both also seemed out of sorts, out of place, temporary occupants of space that Reagan and Clinton inhabited fully. It is instructive to look at news footage of the two two-term presidents and see how oddly similar their body language is: a ninety-degree shoulder less sartorial than spiritual, a springy momentum to the step. A confidence you can see, infectious as flu.

By the time Bob Dole gave up running the Senate to run for president, the voters knew what to look for. Seeing the poor man attempt to trade his semaphore style—"Bob Dole. Gets things done. Knows the ropes"—for some synthetic stump eloquence was painful. Like the good reporter lured into work as an editor, the gifted teacher making the move to principal, Bob Dole was pressured by convention into relinquishing the work he loved in pursuit of a role that didn't suit him. Not pretty, as Bob Dole might have growled. Big defeat.

Which really does bring us back to George W. Bush, whose rise to the highest office has had a certain inexorability not unlike that of Dole, although instead of the forward march of the career ladder his has been the upward thrust of the family tree. The phenomenon of politics as a family business cuts both ways: It can mean a high level of comfort, or a sense of chasing a job that doesn't really fit your talents or experience. The Bush character cuts both ways, too. It's difficult to know which man he will be in the White House, the sharp charmer with a ready quip who hosted advisors on the ranch or the snarky hair trigger with the short attention span who lost New Hampshire because he spent too much time snowmobiling.

He doesn't read much, or think a whole lot about political

theory. He gives a speech as though he's reading someone else's words from a TelePrompTer, which is what he's doing. As governor he spent fewer hours at his desk than your average midlevel bureaucrat, with a long break for a lunchtime run. Even clemency appeals took him only slightly longer than it takes to eat a burger. It could be that, taken together, all this will mean he will come to wonder, deep down, why he ever wanted a job that requires so much oratory, concentration, and isolation.

Or perhaps he will find a way to be happy in his work, delegating to the ghosts of Republican administrations past, reveling in the overview, the big picture, the adulation of the people. Perhaps he will find a way to have what those other two happy men did. Behave as if the shortcomings are nonexistent or insignificant. Magnify the skills through constant exhibition. Make the American people feel good by feeling great, by giving off the glow of a man who is thinking, hot damn, I'm the leader of the free world. Juggle and smile. Smile and juggle.

It's the Cult
of Personality

AUGUST 2000

BROKAW AND BUSH, two guys just standing around talking. Shirtsleeves. Sunshine. Fence posts. Cameras. You get the idea. The candidate was hunkered down at the ranch, going mano a mano for a couple of endless empty minutes with the anchorman. The governor showed off his Yiddish—"kibitzing" was how he described what he was doing with his father, the former president—but the seminal moment was in fluent good-ol'-boy. "I know you are a pretty good fisherman," Bush said to Brokaw, who was angling for the name of the then-unknown vice-presidential nominee. "Yes, you are, and I ain't catching."

Take a good look at that verb, fellow voters, and consider what the meaning of "ain't" ain't. It ain't good English, of course, and it ain't necessarily an entirely natural locution for a graduate of Andover and Yale, even by way of west Texas. What it is is a marker for the most important issue of this election. Relaxed, a little irreverent, down-home: That "ain't" is supposed to commu-

nicate a whole tractor load of material about the Bush personality. And personality is key in election 2000.

Do not confuse this with character. Personality is to character
as icing is to cake, as house is to foundation. If character were
all, Bill Clinton would no longer be president. But his personality is still oddly pleasing to some people, part brainiac, part
Bubba, with bad boy to boot. This has been incredibly frustrating
for the president's opponents, who often reflect, with their blood
pressure dangerously high, on how poor Richard Nixon was cru-
cified for simply obstructing justice and suborning perjury. Ah,
but Nixon was utterly charmless, with that rictus of a grin and
that computer-generated speaking style. The Democrats had the
same frustrations during the Reagan years, when the president's
avuncular manner was the Teflon off which slid the monumental
deficit, the disinherited poor, the disinterest in civil rights. Amid
it all the people said, "I don't know why, I just like the guy."

That's the most indelible phrase in American politics: I just
like the guy. It is, for instance, a misconception that Hillary Clinton is running for the Senate in New York against Rick Lazio.
Hillary Clinton is running against public perceptions of her own
personality. Rick Lazio might as well be an Adirondack chair.
The election will be decided by whether the number of those saying "I like her" is greater than the number of those saying "I hate
her." One Lazio voter was quoted in *The New York Times* as saying, in charming regional vernacular, "Kill the bitch." Which
has little to do with health care policy.

Personality is why Dick Cheney's ascension to the number
two spot on the Republican ticket was initially greeted with
hosannas by the usual suspects. In official Washington, Cheney
is universally considered a WANG; that is, a person about whom
everyone says "What a Nice Guy." This made it easy to over-
look his Cro-Magnon voting record as a congressman. No on the

equal rights amendment. No on banning hollow point bullets. No on a resolution suggesting that the South Africans might want to let Nelson Mandela out of jail. No on Head Start. Cheney got a free pass because he isn't a screamer, because he speaks softly and carries a big right wing, because on television he seems thoughtful and sober.

Television is the best tool of the cult of personality. Think of the Kennedy-Nixon debates, when even in fuzzy monochrome one man came across as confident, charismatic, and cool, and the other as grim, edgy, and mechanical. (TV did not, however, create the cult of personality: Remember all those anecdotes about Lincoln telling funny stories in front of a general store stove.) TV turns politics into a cocktail party after which, in the car on the way home, you find yourself saying to your spouse, "You know, we should see more of the Gores." Pundits like to suggest that this is a shortcoming of the American people, that instead of foreign policy they are more interested in arm's length friendship.

But why should the voters lose their hearts to ideology when candidates have not? Candidate Clinton vowed to lift a ban on gay men and lesbians in the military, then quickly caved and came up with the execrable "don't ask, don't tell." George Bush the elder was once a pro-choice Republican who accurately labeled Ronald Reagan's get-richer-quick fiscal policies "voodoo economics." But that was before Reagan picked him for the second spot, when he cut his principles to fit the ticket. Cheney now says he has second thoughts about the amendment, the bullets, Mandela, and Head Start. (Whew—his wife better hope she doesn't become a political liability!) And Governor Tommy Thompson was all over the tube during the Republican convention, saying the party platform was a prix fixe menu, but everyone was welcome to order à la carte.

What's left is personality. History does not value it highly; for the ages character, vision, and achievement trump a winning manner. But just as they use it to choose their friends, their spouses, the neighbors they invite over for a barbecue, the co-workers they join for lunch, so voters use their impressions of a candidate's personality to choose a president. In the next ninety days millions of people will decide, finally, whether they think Al Gore is rigid and humorless or instead serious and diligent, whether George W. Bush is straight-talking and sure of himself or simply arrogant and tactless. And that will matter. A lot.

The Democrats will talk about experience and intelligence, and there is no doubt that both are critical to real leadership. But they must remember when an experienced president of great intellect named Jimmy Carter debated a former actor named Ronald Reagan a week before the 1980 presidential election. Foreign policy, entitlement programs, nuclear weapons: The air was thick with issues. Yet what everyone remembers from that debate was the moment when the insurgent believed the incumbent was once more distorting his views. "There you go again," Reagan rumbled, his head cocked with a show of reluctant, somehow charming, exasperation. And that was that. People just liked the guy.

The Sins of the Fathers

APRIL 2000

IN THE MIDDLE OF LAST MONTH Cardinal Edward Egan, who leads the hugely influential archdiocese of New York, lamented that the Catholic church was "under siege" and threatened with a situation that might put it "out of business."

Each day brought new revelations of pedophile priests, each morning new stories of young Catholics victimized by the men they had been raised to call "Father." But the cardinal was sounding the alarm about something altogether different. In the midst of the greatest scandal to engulf the Church in his lifetime, he was irate about legislation that would require mandatory health insurance coverage for contraceptives in New York State. His anger brought to mind the Gospel of the Sunday before, in which Jesus gave a blind man back his sight while one of the Pharisees criticized him because he had performed the miracle on the Sabbath.

Missing the point has become the stock-in-trade of many of those who purport to lead the world's Catholics. And they are about to miss it again as they talk of better psychological screening for seminarians, of finally relinquishing the role of prosecutor to actual law enforcement authorities, of ministering to victims and their families, of agonizing over how in the world all this could have happened.

Perhaps they might want to ask the ordinary Catholics who have been too little consulted by the high-handed hierarchy. We understand that in the world of "Father knows best" in which we came of age, all of this was bound to occur. For too many years, the Church evidenced a bizarre preoccupation with sins of the flesh so unrelenting and legendary that, to this day, people will ask if the nuns taught me that patent leather shoes reflect up. (No.) The enforced celibacy of the male priesthood, an invention only of the faith's second millennium, taught a clear lesson: Eschewing human sexuality was the greatest glory of the highest calling. ("Our ideal is not to experience desire at all." Clement of Alexandria, saint.) The ban on contraception, another recent invention, taught that sex could be countenanced only when it could lead to pregnancy. There was no passion or pleasure, only procreation and punishment. Of course, there was power, too, the absolute power of the priest, a man whose psychosexual development often became becalmed in what Eugene Kennedy, the psychologist and former priest, describes as "a child's-garden-of-verses world in seminaries and novitiates," a world customarily entered in adolescence, when most of us are just beginning to learn about the uses and abuses of sexuality.

Out of such preparation, with such sentiments, how could there not be some whose sexual impulses would be perverted into twisted power relationships with children or unformed young adults? "They reached towards children," Kennedy writes, "for children they were themselves." And despite the Church's antipathy toward homosexuality, it was inevitable that most of those victimized would be male. After all, the teachings about ordination and celibacy and the evils of desire had as their subtext a misogyny that would lead any reasonable person to conclude that sex with a female is the lowest form of sexual expression. ("Nothing is so powerful in drawing the spirit of a man downwards as the caresses of a woman." Augustine of Hippo, saint.) Even when a kinder, gentler Catholicism began to flower after Vatican II, pregnancy politics often threatened to crowd out social action, and questions about the ordination of women were sometimes treated like the most unthinkable blasphemy, unclean hands on the eucharistic host.

We didn't understand, some of the bishops say now about the pedophiles among them, moved from parish to parish, fresh choirboys to importune and then hush. We thought they could change. We thought they could be cured. We didn't know. There is so much they didn't know years ago, and yet about which they were so certain. They didn't know what it was to bear and rear a half-dozen children, to turn away at night not because of coldness but because of mother fatigue and pregnancy fear. They didn't know what it was like to drag along in the harness of a dreadful marriage, dying by inches. But, no birth control, they said, no divorce. No self-abuse, no petting, no impure thoughts. The Church of a Jesus who let Mary Magdalene caress his feet threatened to be swamped by an icy sea of sexual prohibition.

The bishops gathered wood for this current conflagration every time they turned away from the human condition to emphasize wayward genitalia. They must be amazed at how harshly they are now judged, after all those years of deference, when they were allowed to make their own laws. Perhaps they sense that they are being judged with the ferocity of those accustomed to being judged harshly themselves. The judgment of divorced Catholics reborn in good marriages ordered not to go to Communion. The judgment of women up all night with sick babies lectured about the sanctity of life. The judgment of hardworking devoted priests who have watched the hierarchy cover up the dirt that sullies them, too. The judgment of now-grown children who have taken to drink, drugs, domestic violence, because of the shadow that Father's wandering hands have cast over their lives.

Now there is some new talk of allowing priests to marry, even the occasional radical suggestion that the notion of ordaining women might be revisited. That's the way, isn't it? As soon as a job is devalued enough, they offer it to us. Perhaps, in this case, too late. ("I don't care to belong to any club that will have me as a member." Groucho of Marx, wise guy.) When the sad stories were told from the pulpit of dwindling vocations, there was always this underlying notion of selfishness, of a smirking guy with a beer and a babe not great enough to give himself up to the service of God. Instead there is now a sense of a priestly way of life so out of balance, so estranged from normal human intercourse that, for some, the rapacious pursuit of altar boys can become normative. The leaders of the Church miss the point. This is not simply about pedophilia. It is about a pathology deep and wide, a pathology that allows blindness to continue as long as the Sabbath is observed.

Lead Us Not

DECEMBER 1994

AS A KID I PRAYED IN SCHOOL. Fast. I can say three Our Fathers in the amount of time it takes to eat a Twinkie. The way you do it is, you run "onearthasitisinheaven" and "leadusnotinto-temptation" all together. It's as rich in meaning as the multiplication tables.

I'm not making light of prayer here, but of so-called school prayer, which bears as much resemblance to real spiritual experience as that freeze-dried astronaut food bears to a nice standing rib roast. From what I remember of praying in school, it was almost an insult to God, a rote exercise in moving your mouth while daydreaming or checking out the cutest boy in the seventh grade that was a far, far cry from soul-searching.

But the current conservative mania for a constitutional amendment guaranteeing school prayer doesn't have much to do with prayer anyway, but with a time, a place, an ethos that praying and pledging allegiance at the beginning of each school day represent. It is an attempt to resuscitate an America that died a natural death and, like most dearly departeds, is now shrouded in the rosy tones of selective memory. As a member of the East Stroudsburg, Pennsylvania, school board said to a local reporter of his support of school prayer: "The country has certainly gone downhill morally since they took it out."

Prayer in the schools represents a return to those good old days. They were days in which twelve-year-olds didn't carry guns, in which children didn't mouth off to their elders, in which divorce was rare and marriages stuck for life, in which condoms stayed in wallets and out of schools. They were also days in which black men were strung up from tall trees, women poured caustic cleansers inside themselves rather than face pregnancy, and nobody talked about Daddy's drinking. Queers were sick, women were irrational, and real men taught their sons to use their fists and never mind about their feelings, what are you, a sissy, boy?

Nobody ever seems to remember that part.

The surface of that America gleamed as bright as a breakfront freshly rubbed with paste wax, with no notice taken of what sort of mess might be inside. Some of it truly shone: Main Street, church suppers, the industry, the neighborliness, the embrace of extended family.

But it was also the America in which parents ruled their children but did not know them, nor the children their parents, in which what was handed down from generation to generation was distance and silence. It was the America in which the family so fine in broadcloth and patent leather sitting in the pew on Sunday could have terrible secrets, but no one would ever know it to look at them.

It's not surprising that when Newt Gingrich, the new Speaker of the House of Representatives, was trumpeting the virtues of orphanages for poor kids, he didn't illustrate his point with the group homes operating today, the arduous actual, the real thing. Gingrich, who wants to make everything old new again, instead chose as the epitome of a happy home for little indigents the 1938 movie *Boys Town*. He was living not only in the past but in a past that only existed on celluloid, a Potemkin village in which only the facade is real. The issue of prayer in schools, which Gingrich supports wholeheartedly, is just such a facade, symbol substituted for substance.

Prayer is personal; by the time a homogenized version can be cooked up to suit most faiths and creeds, it will be distasteful to anyone who takes the soul seriously. Prayer heals; this issue has divided for a long, long time. The family behind one of the landmark suits that found school prayer unconstitutional, *School District of Abington Township v. Schempp*, were tormented by neighbors for heeding the call of conscience. So-called Christians sent abusive letters and made abusive phone calls, dishonoring what they professed to prize.

I only wish a moment of spiritual rote recitation before class would put a halo around the head of a kid, or begin to solve our problems. It would make being a parent, and a citizen, so much easier. But learning to forgive those who trespass against us is not that simple. A state of grace owes more to home than school, and much much more to the early years and the everyday acts than to ninety seconds before classes. Speed-speaking the Lord's Prayer is the least of it.

The Right to Be Ordinary

SEPTEMBER 2000

AT LAST OFFICIAL COUNT nearly five hundred gay and lesbian couples had been united in civil union this summer in Vermont. There were flowers, champagne, brides and brides, grooms and grooms. The sky did not fall. The earth did not split in two. Happy families and happy friends watched happy people pledge their love. Big deal. Ho hum. Yawn.

It's hard sometimes to put your finger on the tipping point of tolerance. It's not usually the Thurgood Marshalls and the Sally Rides, the big headlines and the major stories. It's in the small incremental ways the world stops seeing differences as threatening. It's in the woman at the next desk, the guy behind the counter at the deli. And it's finally happening for gay men and lesbians. They're becoming ordinary. It's not that Ellen DeGeneres and Anne Heche came out and came together; it's that when they broke up they were treated like Meg Ryan and Dennis Quaid.

Sometimes the advances seem at first like setbacks. The Supreme Court decision that the Boy Scouts of America could keep out gay scoutmasters has turned into a pyrrhic victory for scouting. Straight men who were once Eagle Scouts sent back their badges. United Way chapters pulled their financial support. Cities and states that had passed laws prohibiting discrimination based on sexual orientation told scout troops they could no longer use public facilities. Local Boy Scout councils asked the national group to reconsider its decision.

What began as an effort by a gay legal group to protect the rights of gay scouts and scoutmasters also became a movement by straight people who thought the whole thing stunk of simple bigotry. On paper the gay scoutmaster lost; in reality it was scouting officials who took a beating. "Maybe it should be called the Boy Scouts of Certain Americans," one lifelong scout told a local paper in Massachusetts as he sent back his Eagle Scout insignia.

Ruminating on the changes in the national climate in the last ten years, Evan Wolfson of the Lambda Legal Defense and Education Fund, who argued the scoutmaster case with the help of one of the largest collections of amici briefs in Supreme Court history, says, "We've won the war. Now we just need to win the battles."

The war was won in hearts and minds, at school board meetings and on playground benches. Early on, because of the closet and the climate, most straight men and women didn't know anyone who was gay, or didn't know they did. With the AIDS epidemic, what they knew focused on body fluids, sexual practices, and premature death. But in the last decade, with the fight for gay marriage and adoptions, teaching positions and spots as scoutmasters, the image of the gay community has changed to one of ordinary people searching for the ordinary ideal: commitment, love, privacy, work, family. People who, just like heterosexuals, are a good deal more than simply what they do in bed.

The old familiar saws about why discrimination, even revulsion and hatred, are justified have begun to fall away. What remains is largely inchoate or biblical. (Note to interested parties: I already have that verse from Leviticus. Have received it many times. Don't send it again.) The best response to all that suspiciously selective scripture is a goof letter to Dr. Laura Schlessinger making the rounds on the Internet. (Note to the anonymous author: bravo.) It thanks the conservative radio talk show host, who has a loyal following of people who apparently were not yelled at enough as children and are trying to find someone to make up for it, for educating people regarding God's law on homosexuality. But it raises a few questions about biblical passages that seem to be conveniently overlooked:

"Leviticus 25:44 states that I may buy slaves from the nations that are around us. A friend of mine claims that this applies to Mexicans but not Canadians. Can you clarify? I have a neighbor who insists on working on the Sabbath. Exodus 35:2 clearly states he should be put to death. Am I morally obligated to kill him myself? A friend of mine feels that even though eating shellfish is an abomination (Leviticus 11:10), it is a lesser abomination than homosexuality. I don't agree. Can you settle this?"

If there are good laughs, can full equality be far behind? Sure, there is still plenty of prejudice. Even the civil unions in Vermont are only a second-rate kind of marriage, smacking of second-class citizenship. There are still too many gay bias murders, too, and too many committed by young men who feel threatened by the very notion of homosexuality. That's one of the saddest things about the decision by the Boy Scouts, that they send a clear message to those who most need to learn tolerance that homophobia is acceptable, natural, even praiseworthy. (Question for the candidates: The president of the United States is the honorary head of the Boy Scouts of America. Will you refuse the job in light of the organization's exclusion of gay men?)

The Philadelphia Lesbian and Gay Task Force did a survey over the last year that showed that almost one in three gay men and lesbians in Pennsylvania had reported some discrimination in the last year. Those figures differed little from the results of similar surveys done almost a decade ago. That's probably true of women, too, and black Americans, and Latinos, that there is still enough prejudice, both individual and institutional, both subtle and overt, to go around. But there is no doubt that things have changed.

It is almost tangible, the ways in which ordinary people who happen to be gay have become unremarkable. This summer the attention of the entire nation focused on a game show whose desert island participants needed to be physically competent and hugely canny. The guy who won *Survivor* was a gay man. His sexuality was a subordinate clause. He was swamped with endorsement offers and interview requests, and now he's in one of those milk ads. Big deal. Ho hum. Yawn. Oh, and hooray.

The Power of One

APRIL 1993

NOW WE HAVE THE NUMBERS GAME. How many gay people are there in the nation? Ten percent? One percent? Four percent? It depends on whom you ask, what survey you read, how statisticians and sex experts crunch the numbers, which respondents tell the truth and which don't. How many marched in Washington on Sunday for the civil rights of gay men and lesbians? Three hundred thousand? Half a million? A million or more? It depends on whether you ask the park police or the march organizers.

But at some level none of it matters at all.

I know that gay men and lesbians have ample reason to believe their political clout in America, the most quantifying of countries, will be measured by their numbers. I know, too, that those who want to prove that homosexuality is a "deviant lifestyle" are anxious to show that the demands are disproportionate to the number of demanders, as though the right to be treated fairly depended on a head count.

But it's the power of one that really brings change. No one's head is truly turned around by a faceless sea of folks seen from a distance marching on the capital, or by numbers on sexual behavior from a research center.

It's the power of one that does it.

It's the power of one man like Sergeant Jose Zuniga, who was the Sixth Army's 1992 soldier of the year and a medic in the Gulf War. Before the march he stood before the television cameras and so before the world and said, with a chestful of medals, that he was proud to be a soldier, and he was proud to be gay.

Right that minute, maybe, some fellow vets and fellow Americans wrote him off. But there have to be people who have worked with him, trained with him, fought with him, who are now forced to reexamine their attitudes toward gay men, to compare their prejudices with what they know of this one individual.

Maybe in the beginning those people will decide that Sergeant Zuniga is the exception, and that the rule is that gay men are predatory, effeminate, unfit for service. They may embrace the old "Okay, but . . ." analysis, which we have seen with blacks, with Latinos, with women and now with gay people. It goes like this: "Jose is okay, but the rest of them . . ."

Stereotypes fall in the face of humanity. You toodle along, thinking that all gay men wear leather after dark and should never, ever be permitted around a Little League field. And then one day your best friend from college, the one your kids adore, comes out to you. Or that wonderful woman who teaches third grade is spotted leaving a lesbian bar in the next town.

And the ice of your closed mind begins to crack.

Day by day, this is how the world will change for gay men and lesbians, with the power of one—one person who doesn't fit into the straight world's fact pattern and so alters it a tiny bit, irrevocably. A revered actor who was typecast in tough-guy roles. A beloved female friend who cannot be transformed into a hate object. Coming out is a powerful thing.

It is why the march, one of the biggest civil rights demonstrations in the history of this country, was most powerful when it reflected not quantity, but quality. A sunburned man in chinos. Two silver-haired women hand in hand, smiling. A woman pushing a stroller. Sure, there were men in lipstick and women in buzz cuts. And women in lipstick and men in buzz cuts. Like straight people, gay people are a diverse group. To paraphrase Gloria Steinem on turning fifty, this is what gay looks like.

In recent years gay men and lesbians have moved purposefully ahead in the civic arena, putting money behind candidates, crafting antidiscrimination legislation, demanding that their relationships be formally recognized. No matter what their numbers, they've become a formidable political force.

But a veneer of tolerance atop a deep pool of hatred, distrust, and estrangement is no more than a shiny surface, as civil rights leaders can testify from decades of experience. The numbers in Washington were not as important as the faces, the sheer humanity of one person after another stepping forward, saying: Look at me. I am a cop, a mother, a Catholic, a Republican, a soldier, an American. So the ice melts. The hate abates. The numbers, finally, all come down to one.

Smoke Gets in Your Eyes

JULY 2000

IMAGINE THAT MILLIONS OF AMERICANS are addicted to a lethal drug. Imagine that the Food and Drug Administration has repeatedly ducked its responsibility by refusing to regulate that drug. And imagine that when the FDA finally does its duty, an appeals court decides that it cannot do so, that the drug is so dangerous that if the FDA regulated it, it would have to be banned.

Welcome to the topsy-turvy world of tobacco, where nothing much makes sense except the vast profits, where tobacco company executives slip-slide along the continuum from aggrieved innocence to heartfelt regret without breaking a sweat, and where the only people who seem to be able to shoot straight are the jurors who decide the ubiquitous lawsuits.

The most recent panel to do the right thing handed down a judgment of $145 billion on behalf of sick smokers in the state of Florida, the largest jury damage award in history. Lawyers for the tobacco companies thundered that the award would bankrupt them, yet the stock market scarcely shuddered. Experts said the amount would likely to be reduced when cooler judicial heads prevailed.

The jurors, who gave up two years of their lives, listened to endless witnesses, and yet were able to hammer the tobacco companies after deliberating only a few hours, could be forgiven if they felt they'd fallen down Alice's rabbit hole into Wonderland, where the Red Queen cries "Off with their heads" but no one is ever executed. Al Gore, for instance, insisted not long ago that he will do everything he can to keep cigarettes out of the hands of children, inspired by the death of his own sister from lung cancer. But he says he would never outlaw cigarettes because millions of people smoke. Here is a question: How many users mandate legality? What about the 1.5 million cocaine users, or the estimated 2.4 million people who shoot or snort heroin?

I can almost feel all the smokers out there, tired of standing outside their office buildings puffing in the rain when once they could sit comfortably at their desk, jumping up and down and yelling, "Tobacco is different from illicit drugs!" Because it is legal? Now there's a circular argument. A hundred years ago the sale of cigarettes was against the law in fourteen states. The Supreme Court, which ruled earlier this year that the FDA did not have the power to regulate tobacco, upheld a Tennessee law outlawing the sale of cigarettes in 1900. The justices agreed with a state court that had concluded, "They possess no virtue but are inherently bad and bad only." At the time, Coca-Cola still contained cocaine, and heroin was in cough syrups.

Since then the tables have turned. Tobacco companies spread political contributions around like weed killer on the lawn in summer, although they've passed from their bipartisan period into an era when they support largely complicit Republicans, who like free enterprise (and soft money) more than they hate emphysema. (George W. Bush, perhaps mindful of the punishing cost of a presidential campaign, responded to a question about the recent mega-settlement by bemoaning a litigious nation.) Responsibility-minded Americans accept the argument that individuals have the right to poison themselves, although studies showing that the vast majority of smokers began as minors raise questions about informed consent. Official tobacco apologists spent years insisting their product did not cause cancer, then that it was not addictive. Now they've done a 180, arguing that since there is no such thing as a safe cigarette, a government agency like the FDA, created to regulate the safety of products, cannot touch them.

If this sounds like having it both ways, that's because it is. Philip Morris launders money by making large contributions to nonprofit organizations, soup kitchens and ballet companies and museums and shelters, being a good citizen with the profits of a product that kills 400,000 people a year. And magazines run articles about the dangers of cigarettes in the same issues that advertise them.

Even tobacco foes have fudged. When Dr. David Kessler ran the FDA, he publicly concluded what everyone already knew: that cigarettes are nothing more than a primitive delivery device for nicotine, a dangerous and addictive drug. But the agency balked at taking the next step. The Food, Drug, and Cosmetic Act forbids the sale of any drug that is not safe and effective, and part of the FDA's mandate is to regulate devices. Cigarettes are a device. The drug they deliver is patently unsafe. Banning cigarette sales is the only logical conclusion.

That's not going to happen in our lifetime, which is why even a more aggressive FDA refused to take this to the limit. Too many tobacco farmers, too many tobacco addicts; a right to a livelihood, a right to a lifestyle. (Both of these arguments hold for legalizing illicit drugs as well, but never mind.) Prohibition is a dirty word in America. But tobacco can in no way be compared to alcohol. Many people can and do drink safely and in moderation, while it is impossible to smoke without some pernicious health effects, and nearly all smokers can be described as addicts. But if cigarettes were outlawed, what to do with all those tobacco junkies? Nicotine clinics providing the patch, strong coffee, and hypnotherapy?

Public service announcements, catchy commercials for kids, settlements with the states to recover health care costs: The tobacco companies, who once swore they were doing nothing wrong, are now willing to lose some ideological battles to win the war of the profit margin. One Philip Morris executive appearing at a recent conference even told Dr. Kessler, whose efforts to restrict sales and advertising aimed at children spawned a battle royal of billable hours, that he welcomed "serious regulation of the tobacco industry at the federal level." Now they tell us. Why shouldn't the Marlboro men play the angles; the public and the pols have provided them with so many angles to play. Here is the bottom line: Cigarettes are the only legal product that, when used as directed, cause death. The rest is just a puppet show in the oncology wing.

17 Going on 18

NOVEMBER 1994

Dear Golden Girl,

Got a letter from your mom the other day. Her description did you proud: "At seventeen she is at the high end of meeting every parent's expectations, including mine," she wrote. "An A student, captain of the tennis team, president of her high school service organization."

But her tone was despondent, disappointed, and angry. You've started to smoke, and she wants me to persuade you to stop.

That's not the way it works. Seventeen or seventy, people quit smoking when they've convinced themselves it's the right thing to do. But there are a couple of things I can mention.

There's the guy you may fall in love with someday who thinks kissing a smoker is as seductive as licking the bottom of a dirty ashtray. There are the babies you might want to have and the damage you could do to them in utero if you are so addicted to cigarettes that you can't quit when you're pregnant.

There are the yellow fingers and the yellow teeth. Your clothes smell. So does your hair. It gets harder to stop every day.

In this very newspaper we ran a photograph of two fashion industry types wearing T-shirts that are part of a campaign to combat breast cancer. They were holding bottles of designer water in one hand and cigarettes in the other. The mixed messages you receive are confusing.

There's nothing confusing about smoking for me. I remember the day of the rehearsal dinner for Jim and Mary's wedding, when my father-in-law picked me up at the bus stop, his voice whittled away to a faint rasp. A cold, he said. Laryngitis. A year later he was dead of lung cancer, still smoking up to the end.

Bill Cahan, the surgeon who has been an inveterate opponent of the tobacco industry, sent me a photograph of a diseased lung. It looks like an alien life form in a bad sci-fi movie. He says I should remind you that smokers who take the Pill face an increased risk of hardening of the arteries, stroke, and heart disease, and that tongue cancer is on the rise.

Joe Cherner, who founded an antismoking advocacy group, says I should mention that you're being manipulated by the middle-aged. "There's an entire group of adults whose careers depend on getting you to start smoking by deception," he says. More than 400,000 people will die because of cigarettes this year. You're part of the next wave, the new wave, of consumers, patients, fatalities. Welcome to the oncology floor.

And meet Janet Sackman, who remembers seventeen as if it were yesterday.

"When I was seventeen I had the world in my hands," she says, and she's not exaggerating. She was a successful model: soap and swimsuit ads, the covers of *Life* and *Look*. In 1949 they stood her on skis in a studio with phony mountains in the background and a fan blowing her blond hair and made her the Lucky Strike girl. There was just one catch: "An executive for the tobacco people said to me, 'It would be a good idea for you to learn how to smoke. That way you'll look authentic.' "

So at just your age Janet learned to smoke. She went on to do Chesterfield ads on television—"You know, he's right!" she enthused when the announcer said that Chesterfield left no unpleasant aftertaste—and to marry and have four children. In 1983 she had her larynx removed and in 1990 she lost part of one lung.

She still looks great but she doesn't sound so good. Her voice box gone, she had to learn to talk all over again, burping air through a hole in her esophagus just above the collarbone. It took her about six months to say her first word; now she teaches others the technique.

"I cough through that hole, I sneeze through that hole, and I talk through that hole," she says in a mechanical croak. "I can't make any sound when I laugh or cry. I can't be sarcastic and I can't tell a joke. I have the same monotone speech all the time."

"And I'm one of the fortunate ones," she added, "because I'm alive. I wish I had realized how important my life was when I was seventeen. Tell her the single most important thing to do for your looks and your life, the single most important thing, is not to smoke. If she could hear me speak, she'd listen."

Your mother says you have a birthday coming up. Here's Janet Sackman's suggestion for what you could give yourself as a gift: many many more.

The Call from
the Governor

JUNE 2000

THE MIASMA OF SEXUAL DETRITUS that has swirled around Bill Clinton as though he were some grown-up variant of the Peanuts character Pig Pen began in earnest on the national stage in January 1992. That was when the supermarket tabloid the *Star* introduced the electorate to Gennifer Flowers. Her tale of good loving gone bad eventually spawned a *Penthouse* pictorial, a lackluster career as a lounge singer, the first wave of tasteless Clinton jokes, and a public discussion of what was known as the character issue.

But at the same time that Ms. Flowers's story of a twelve-year affair appeared at the checkout counter, right next to the gum and the Tic Tacs, Mr. Clinton was failing a test of character infinitely more important and exacting. While everyone still remembers Gennifer with a G, there is collective amnesia about Rickey Ray Rector, whose notoriety peaked at about the same time, but less spectacularly.

Rickey Ray Rector killed a police officer, then literally blew his own brains out. The surgery that saved his life left him with what one doctor called "the mind of a six-year-old," but a six-year-old who barked like a dog, thought there were alligators in his jail cell, and had no memory of the events that led him to Arkansas's death row. Rickey Ray was so out to lunch that even the warden was shaken by his death sentence. Then-governor Clinton apparently was not. Trailing accusations of adultery, he left the campaign trail and went home to Little Rock, on the scene when a man as mentally incompetent as a man could be was executed. The juggernaut that suggested that Clinton was morally suspect because he'd had sex with a woman not his wife rolled on, leaving Rickey Ray a whisper in the clamoring of the vox populi.

We have chosen to judge public servants on sex and drugs instead of life and death, so they can scarcely be blamed for following our lead and taking the cheap and easy way. Perhaps it is simpler to assess concupiscence than conscience. The first gives us the candidates we can manage to stomach, the second those we are obliged to admire. In the crucible of the death penalty, there is a unique opportunity to know what they are made of, their public faces pressed up against the terrible one-way mirror of mortality. Yet we scarcely seem to notice.

The issue has always been debated with arguments that work the margins and conveniently ignore the core. Deterrence, public support, righteous revenge: All warily circle the underlying problem, which is that capital punishment is the endgame of a system run by humans, and therefore will always be subject to human error. Anyone who honestly considers the witches' brew of sometimes overzealous prosecutors and police, incompetent or overworked defense counsel, and racial and class bias in capital cases would have to admit that error is inevitable. As capital punishment became seen as some panacea—when really it was a placebo—public officials who knew better chose to avert their eyes.

That is no longer possible. Science has been given credit because of advances in DNA testing, testing that can use evidence to nab the guilty and eliminate the innocent, even the innocent who have already been sentenced to die for crimes they did not commit. But it is really the character of one elected official that has turned the capital punishment debate on its head. God bless Governor George Ryan of Illinois. Faced with the astonishing statistical news that more people on the state's death row were being exonerated than executed, he instituted a moratorium. Though the governor is a conservative Republican and a death penalty advocate, he has said he doubts anyone else will be executed during his term.

This contrasts sharply with the response of Governor George W. Bush of Texas, who during the last five years has overseen a kind of execution assembly line in which 131 inmates have died through lethal injection. The Republican presidential candidate says, "I'm confident that every person that's been put to death under our state has been guilty of the crime charged."

Any demographer would wonder how Illinois wound up with a staggering thirteen men exonerated against twelve executed, while Texas, tenfold, had managed to make no mistakes. Are Texas juries cannier or fairer? Do Texas prosecutors make fewer errors, Texas defenders work harder than their counterparts in Illinois? Certainly there are notable differences in character between the two governors. Ryan seems a man humbled and horrified by the possibility of error, "the ultimate nightmare, the state's taking of innocent human life." Bush, on the other hand, last year made fun in an interview of a double murderer who had found God in prison and asked for executive clemency. He imitated Karla Faye Tucker's request in a mocking whimper: "Please don't kill me."

It is worth mentioning that that glimpse into the darkest side of the governor's middle school persona was shockingly underpublicized. It appeared in the first issue of *Talk* magazine, its fire stolen by sex, by a Hillary Clinton profile that was described in press shorthand—inaccurately, if you read the whole story—as an apologia for Bill's womanizing based on his difficult childhood. At the time the biggest question about the character of Bush the younger was whether he'd ever used cocaine.

(Personally, I'd vote for a former cokehead over the kind of guy who makes fun of dead women any day of the week.)

It's unlikely that many major political figures will have the guts to oppose the death penalty; there's no Election Day premium in it, since most Americans have been taken in by the placebo effect. But the least they can do is approach the act of taking the life of another with the awe, the respect, and the special care that it deserves. While we were worrying about casual drug use, Bush was being casually cruel about a woman pleading for her life. His response showed an immaturity that is a singular defect in character. While we were wondering how Hillary felt about Gennifer, Clinton was turning his back on a man who was a poster child for executive clemency. His lack of response showed a finger-to-the-wind affect that is a singular defect in character. Maybe both of them figured we wouldn't notice. And we didn't.

Indivisible? Wanna Bet?

JULY 2002

EVERY YEAR SOMEBODY OR OTHER finds a way to show that American kids are ignorant of history. The complaint isn't that they don't know the broad strokes, the rationale the South gave for keeping slaves, the ideas behind the New Deal. It's always dates and names, the game show questions that ask what year the Civil War began and who ordered the bombing of Hiroshima, the stuff of the stand-up history bee.

But if American adults want to give American kids a hard time about their dim knowledge of the past and how it's reflected in the present, they might first become reasonable role models on the subject. And the modeling could begin with the members of Congress, who with few exceptions went a little nuts when an appeals court in California ruled that the phrase "under God" in the Pledge of Allegiance was unconstitutional.

I don't really know whether that is an impermissible breach of the firewall between church and state. The proper boundaries twixt secular and sacred have been argued long and hard by legal minds more steeped in the specific intricacies than my own. But I do know this: Attempts to make the Pledge sound like a cross between the Ten Commandments and the Constitution are laughable, foolish, and evidence of the basest sort of political jingoism.

So let's go to the history books, as citizens of this country so seldom do. The Pledge of Allegiance started in 1892 as a set piece in a magazine, nothing more, nothing less. It was written by a man named Francis Bellamy in honor of Columbus Day, a holiday that scarcely exists anymore except in department store sales. The words "under God" were nowhere in it, hardly surprising since Bellamy had been squeezed out of his own church the year before because of his socialist leanings. His daughter said he would have hated the addition of the words "under God" to a statement he envisioned uniting a country divided by race, class, and, of course, religion.

Those two words went into the Pledge just fifty years ago, and for the most deplorable reason. It was the height of the Red Scare in America, when the lives of those aligned or merely flirting with the Communist Party were destroyed by paranoia, a twisted strain of uberpatriotism, and the machinations of Senator Joseph McCarthy, for whom an entire vein of baseless persecution is now named. Contrary to the current political argument that "under God" is not specifically devout, the push to put it in the Pledge was mounted by the Knights of Columbus, a Catholic men's organization, as an attempt to counter "godless communism." President Eisenhower signed a bill making this law, saying that the words would help us to "remain humble."

Humility had nothing to do with it. We are not a humble people. Instead the Pledge had become a little litmus test. The words "under God" were a way to indicate that America was better than other nations—we were, after all, under the direct protection of the Deity—and adding them to the Pledge was another way of excluding, of saying that believers were real Americans and skeptics were not. Would any member of Congress have been brave enough at that moment to say that a Pledge of Allegiance that had been good enough for decades was good enough as it stood?

Would any member of Congress, in the face of the current spate of unquestioning flag-waving, have been strong enough to eschew leaping to his feet and pressing his hand over his heart, especially knowing the percentage of atheist voters is in the low single digits? Well, there were a few, a few who said the decision was likely to be overturned anyhow, a few who said there were more pressing matters before the nation, a few who were even willing to agree with the appeals court that "under God" probably did not belong in the Pledge in a country founded on a righteous division between government and religion.

But most of the rest went wild. Even Senator Clinton invoked "divine providence," even Senator Feinstein called the court decision "embarrassing." What was embarrassing was watching all those people, Republicans, Democrats, liberals, conservatives, shout "under God" on the Senate floor, as though government was a pep rally and they were on the sanctified squad. Senator Bob Smith of New Hampshire had this to say: "If you don't believe there's a God, that's your privilege, but it is still a nation under God." Huh?

I have a warm personal relationship with God; I often picture her smiling wryly and saying, in the words of Shakespeare's Puck, "Lord, what fools these mortals be!" Or perhaps something less fond. Now, as fifty years ago, a nation besieged by ideological enemies requires nuanced and judicious statecraft and instead settles for sloganeering, demonizing, and politicking. One senator said after the court decision was handed down that the Founding Fathers must be spinning in their graves. The person who must be spinning is poor Francis Bellamy, who wanted to believe in an inclusive utopia and instead became in our time the father of convenient rhetoric.

The Sounds of Silence

APRIL 2003

LAST MONTH A UNITED WAY CHAPTER in Florida disinvited the actress Susan Sarandon from a fund-raising luncheon at which she'd agreed to speak. This was scarcely surprising. Many charities are happy to use celebrities to attract donors to their events, but they like them to be as decorative and inoffensive as the flower centerpieces. And with war looming, the Oscar-winning actress, who has been outspokenly liberal on a variety of social issues and consistently critical of the invasion of Iraq, must have suddenly seemed akin to a cactus.

It was an early salvo in the difficult and painful war here at home. The rules of engagement were clear. If you had early doubts about the use of American power in Iraq, you should sit down and shut up because you might imperil the eventual result. If you continued to have doubts about our foreign policy while the war was ongoing, you should sit down and shut up because you were giving aid and comfort to the enemy.

And, trust me: If you still have doubts about the wisdom of

unilateral action now, you should sit down and shut up because we won.

Never mind if you are asking yourself why a nation we were told was lousy with chemical and biological weapons never used them during a punishing bombardment. Never mind if you are asking yourself why the oft-invoked but never factually supported ties between Saddam and Al Qaeda didn't lead to the predicted terrorist attacks in the United States.

Sit down, you're rocking the boat.

The bright side of this is that it offers a valuable lesson in American history. Each time the United States becomes imperial, it betrays the very keystone upon which its greatness rests. It suppresses dissent and suggests that national interest is more important than free speech. In the wake of its primacy after World War II, this became so pernicious that lives were ruined, not only by Communist Party membership, but also by third-hand suggestions of it. Only a decade that put the lid on discourse as tightly as the fifties could have exploded into the free association of the sixties.

The division between those who support the Iraqi war and those who do not has become an unbridgeable ravine of accusation and name-calling, as fraught an issue as this country has had since it first discovered abortion. The greatness of America is almost unrecognizable in the resulting maelstrom. Its most basic principles are mangled, when, in places like Albany, New York, a man is arrested at a mall for wearing a T-shirt with the biblical legend PEACE ON EARTH on the front and the musical legend GIVE PEACE A CHANCE on the back. (The mall has a policy that bans patrons from wearing clothing "with slogans that may incite a disturbance." Let's hope no one ever comes in with a shirt that reads FREE BEER IN THE FOOD COURT.)

The all-purpose accusation against dissenters is "unpatriotic," deeply ironic since those first patriots are celebrated for rebelling against government policies they considered wrong. Children learn of the greatness of those who spoke out against the policies of George III, then hear vilified those who do not agree with George W. How confusing. Almost as confusing as seeing your parents glued to *Access Hollywood* and then hearing them complain they can't understand why celebrities believe anyone would pay attention to anything they have to say.

If the free exchange of ideas is temporarily suspended in the interest of "supporting our troops" (as though all soldiers are also of one mind about foreign policy), then what is the gift we bring to the Iraqi people? Old Navy fleece? Stuffed crust pizza? Much of what we have to export as a nation is similarly transient, except for this: the right to elect leaders, to watch what they do through the vehicle of a free press, and then, if we choose, to damn them for doing it, in coffeehouses, at home, from the steps of the courthouse or the statehouse, in private and in public, too. If there is any justification for an imperial America, it is because this is the jewel in its crown.

Last week the war at home continued unabated; the president of the Baseball Hall of Fame, a former Reagan press secretary, canceled an anniversary screening of the film *Bull Durham* because it stars Sarandon and her equally uncompliant companion, Tim Robbins. In a letter he made the incendiary, baseless, and, given his past life, clearly partisan accusation that the failure of two actors to go along with a policy they cannot support puts American soldiers in harm's way.

"May we never confuse honest dissent with disloyal subversion." A line from Robbins's irate reply to the baseball guy? Nah, it's Eisenhower at a time when the Constitution was mutilated by McCarthy and his minions, and dissent and subversion were constantly confused. And so it is in our time. If, in the shadow of the unilateralist power niche the United States will occupy in the foreseeable future, its citizens are pressured by their government, their communities, and their neighbors to speak with one cautious voice, we will have saved Iraq and damned ourselves. In a democratic society, the only treason is silence.

The Great Obligation

APRIL 2004

IN 1981 I INTERVIEWED A COUPLE named Stanley and Julie Patz. Perhaps the last name rings a bell. Twenty-five years ago, their six-year-old son, Etan, left his family's lower-Manhattan loft for the schoolbus stop two blocks away and vanished. This was before pictures on milk cartons, or Amber Alerts, or even the National Center for Missing & Exploited Children, which Etan's disappearance helped create. Stan Patz is a photographer, and a picture he had taken of his son, bright eyes, long bangs, became iconic overnight. Etan Patz: the most famous missing child since the Lindbergh baby.

"We're not interested in publicity anymore," Stan Patz said when I called.

He didn't remember the story I had done; I've never forgotten it. The couple's loss, their need, their grief, made me feel that I had to lift the level of my game to meet the level of their bereavement. This was impossible, but I was moved to try.

I have often thought about the effect the Patzes had on me as some reporters have brought disgrace upon the profession. And it has made me wonder whether good journalists always have that moment in their background, the moment that merges humanity and story in an indelible way. Or the opposite: Are the frauds always of character, not craft? Skimming Jayson Blair's sloppy and unrepentant book about his confabulations at *The New York Times,* I sensed no concern for the people he covered. His emphasis was on quantity, how many stories he could shoehorn into the shortest span of days. The individuals in his stories were never more than the means to a careerist end.

How else to explain the actions of Jack Kelley, the *USA Today* star reporter who resigned amid an investigation that concluded he had invented significant parts of at least eight articles? One of his suspect stories—an account of an escape from Cuba in a small boat under a crescent moon that was not out on the night in question amid a storm that never occurred—was illustrated with a photo Kelley had taken of a woman he called Yacqueline. (The names of the alleged human beings changed several times as Kelley worked on his draft.) In his account, Yacqueline and her young son tragically drowned. In real life, the woman in the photograph is alive and living in the United States, a legal immigrant. No boat, no moon. Not quite so page one, that.

Reporters are often asked about their obligation to readers, but perhaps the most important obligation is the one we owe the subjects of our stories, whose lives are limned by our words, for better or for worse. David Halberstam, the bestselling author who won a Pulitzer telling the truth about Vietnam, says it was writing obituaries as a young man at the Nashville *Tennessean* that made this clear to him. "For most people it was the one time they got their name in print," he recalled. "If you got something wrong, you could cause enormous pain to ordinary people."

Tom Brokaw, the NBC anchorman, remembers a young black woman who decided to march in the streets of Americus, Georgia, during dangerous racial unrest there. "I'm often asked to name my most memorable interview," Brokaw says, "and I suppose most people think I'll say Dr. Martin Luther King or Bobby Kennedy or Gorbachev or Mandela or Margaret Thatcher or some other big name. But honestly, I always bring up that young woman. I was just twenty-five at the time and she taught me so much that night."

Perhaps that sort of learning curve is harder now. Ordinary people too often are turned into celebrities, so that Jessica Lynch, whose story was one of those Blair phonied up, went from a soldier from West Virginia to a national figure faster than you could say "made-for-TV movie." The Patzes predate the strafe heartbreaker, those human-interest stories transmuted into all-pathos-all-the-time, their protagonists hurtling from one newsmagazine to another until they seem less like people and more like talking heads. And talking heads never inspire compassion.

All this makes you wonder if journalism schools should teach not just accuracy, but empathy. But the truth is, you really get that by covering stories, not studying them, by imagining yourself in the place of the people you interview. All these years later, and I still apologized to Stan for talking about his son in the past tense. "I got over that a long time ago," he said. "He's gone."

He's not looking for publicity anymore. His son has been declared legally dead by the courts; Stan Patz believes Etan was murdered by a convicted child molester now in jail in Pennsylvania. Still there's a pad by the phone for taking notes when someone calls, most recently a woman who believes her former husband is Etan. Still he clips the stories out of habit. The original impulse is gone: "To create a history for Etan." If you're a reporter, I leave you with that image for those times when you think what you do is fleeting. The closest thing this man has to the body of his son is the body of your work. If that doesn't make you want to do better, find another job.

3 Body

THE WOMAN THING CAME WITH THE TERRITORY, and with the chromosomes. In the beginning it was something of a big deal. The first woman this, the only woman that. As one of the first New York City female firefighters said as one of her fellows (females?) was promoted, "All of these firsts, you hope that they won't be the lasts."

I wrote about those women when they were first fighting to get on the force. In some ways it seems a long time ago, in some ways just part of the ubiquitous gender scenery.

The woman thing was my birthright and my great advantage. That last is the part I was not supposed to admit when I started out. I was an affirmative action hire at *The New York Times,* one of many responses to a class action suit who arrived in the slightly grubby newsroom cloaked in confidence, redolent of terror. In the years after, after I had been an editor and become a columnist, I was always asked how bad the treatment had been, how pernicious the sexism. Friends had discovered they were making less than their male counterparts and being steered away from certain stories. Neither of those things happened to me. The day I was sent up in a single engine plane over the Adirondacks to look for a crash site for the sake of a color story, I wished as I vomited into a plastic bag that someone had thought to handle me with kid gloves. No one had. No one had handled me, period. I had no stories to tell of sexual harassment or discrimination.

Instead I wound up a so-called lifestyle columnist, with a beat that was the richest, the most interesting, probably the most important, and surely the simplest I had ever had. My body, myself, my kids, my friends. The glass ceiling, the labor room, the first lady, the White House. Whenever I gave speeches about the position of women in America, I had to keep revising them. The CEO count. The numbers in the Senate. There were not enough, but there were more and more and more each year. When finally one day I asked my daughter whether she had ever thought she would prefer to be a boy, she replied, "I think it would be too boring."

That is what I had thought, growing up, about being a woman. The life of housework and child-rearing that most women I knew inhabited (and the life of secretarial work and painfully neat one-bedroom apartments that the few career women I knew had) seemed so stupefyingly dull that when I considered them in terms of my own future I got a feeling not unlike vertigo, except that instead of my head spinning it ground to a stop. But I liked the notion of battling adversity and rising triumphant. It was not until I had been in the game for a couple of years that I realized that adversity had already been battled by the women a generation older than I was, and that what was left for me was an overwhelming richness.

I don't mean to be a Pollyanna about this. When I gave a speech to a women's political action group in Minnesota, they

handed out postcards that told the story in simple graphics better than any words could say: little blocks representing the members of Congress, the nation's governors, the presidency. Men in
blue, women in red, and the red blocks were few and far between. You have only to watch a couple of music videos to know
that it is still possible, and commonplace, to think of women as
sexual objects, mainly a frame to transport breasts and genitalia.
You have only to consider the way Hillary Clinton has become
both a heroine and an object of extraordinary hatred to know that
power in the female is still fraught, particularly for the male.

But you have only to consider that Hillary has been both first
lady and U.S. senator (and mother and betrayed wife and lawyer)
to detect a deep and enduring change in all of our lives. You
could feel it when more men began to stay home and care for
their children while their wives earned a living, or when the
movement to support girls in schools was taken up on the distaff
side, and complaints began about how boys were being short-
changed.

We've lived through the greatest period of change for women
in the history of planet Earth. That's pretty astonishing to contemplate, but it was fantastic to cover. From young women playing quarterback on high school football teams to older women
trading in their empty nests for city council seats, from young
women trying new methods of contraception to older ones refusing hormone replacement therapy, from young women insisting
they could be sexual beings and still be treated seriously to older
women saying the same: Things happened so fast you almost got
history whiplash.

By the time the dust had settled we had more choices than
we knew what to do with. The fact that this was presented as a
problem—"Can You Really Have It All?" might as well have been
programmed into the computers of women's magazine editors—

said more than anything about how revolutionary this was, and how uncomfortable revolutions always make even those who benefit. As it said on the tip cup in one coffee bar in New York, IF YOU CAN'T DEAL WITH CHANGE, LEAVE IT HERE.

I wouldn't change a thing. I've borne a daughter into the most exciting world for women imaginable. Perhaps because of that she is a person with a highly developed sense of adventure and a sense of entitlement, too. No one had better try to hold out on her. As for wanting to be male, well, she came along just when that option seemed like settling for less.

The Reasonable
Woman Standard

MARCH 2000

THIS MAY SOUND STRANGE coming from a lifelong feminist, but I've had it with Women's History Month. It's hard for me to believe that Betty Friedan wrote *The Feminine Mystique*, protesters trashed the Miss America Pageant, and countless women hazarded class action suits so that each March fourth graders could learn fun facts about Eleanor Roosevelt. Sometimes it seems to me the event is just a sad symbol of how little change we were willing to settle for. A month? We ought to get most of the year.

Sure, I get the point: I made it through girlhood without ever hearing of Sojourner Truth or Marie Curie, and I am willing to acknowledge progress. Nearly half the medical students in the country are female. So is the secretary of state. Girls play ice hockey in the Olympics. No one blinks at the sight of a woman cop. Fewer parents believe that their sons should check out colleges and their daughters check out catering halls. Rapes are reported, even prosecuted. Everything has changed since I was a girl, when my choice of career was either mother or nun.

And some things never change. The advocacy organization Girls Incorporated releases a survey of schoolgirls this week with the following results: 63 percent said "girls are under a lot of pressure to please everyone," 65 percent said "girls are expected to spend a lot of time on housework and taking care of younger brothers and sisters," and more than half said that "girls are expected to speak softly and not cause trouble." And why not? Last week three young men were convicted of manslaughter after slipping the date rape drug GHB into the drink of a fifteen-year-old girl who died. One said this was to make the party "lively." Translated: The best woman is an unconscious woman.

So much for Sally Ride.

The truth is that we got stuck on a plateau here, somewhere between change, which is good, and transformation, which is excellent. There has been some transformation, thanks to the women's movement, which is now, like God, everywhere, from Little League to the Supreme Court. Why do patients feel more confident in asking questions of their physicians and seeking alternative care? Why has community policing, in which cops try to know those they serve, become the order of the day in many cities? Why do newspaper and magazine stories more often include human beings along with statistics? Is it coincidence that all this has happened since women began to enter those professions as both active participants and informed consumers in ever-greater numbers?

I don't think so.

But transformation has come slowly, and too often American society has remained like those men's schools that admitted women, and overnight became—men's schools with women. A new book, *A Law of Her Own*, an utterly persuasive argument for replacing the reasonable person legal standard (which is really just a reasonable man standard in mufti) with a reasonable woman standard for certain crimes, sums up the plateau perfectly: "To be treated the same means to be treated the same as men." The two lawyers who wrote the book, Caroline Forell and Donna Matthews, argue that applying the test of how a reasonable woman would behave and react in adjudicating crimes like rape, domestic violence, and sexual harassment is only sensible because men frequently see those offenses quite differently than the women who are their habitual victims.

The advantage of this is not only that it is better for women, but that it is better for everyone. "Applying the reasonable woman standard when a woman sexually harasses a man treats his injury more seriously and respectfully than under a reasonable person/man standard," the authors write. Legal standards that suggest that men can't help being boorish and predatory may deny women justice, but they also deny men dignity. That more female professors than their male counterparts are attracted to the profession because of teaching rather than research is better for students—of both genders. That female doctors have taken the lead in supporting the health care consumer movement is good for patients—of both genders.

The values of big business too often remain old-fashioned values of hierarchical management and rigid arrangements. If female managers are more collaborative and flexible—and some studies show they are—then all workers benefit when those women help set the agenda. But in many companies that model is not rewarded. In many tenure decisions teaching is not rewarded. In many hospitals patient contact is not rewarded. A reasonable woman standard may be better for consumers in countless areas. But it's devalued by custom.

In the recent past, the result of combining that custom with feminist change was sometimes women living imitation guys' lives. Of course many of us couldn't manage the masquerade because the most important transformation, the one in which everyone would share domestic duties, never came off, leaving many women with two jobs, one at the office, the other at home. Martha Stewart's grapevine wreaths notwithstanding, housework is mainly scut work and there is no argument beyond the simple demands of fairness that can suggest that men will be enriched by loading the dishwasher. But when women do most of the child-rearing—and they do—men miss the most important emotional experience of their own lives. That's tragic—and bad for all.

Where the standards of reasonable women are honored, the culture has improved. Where they are not, not. In 1970, when she was trying without success to sell the equal rights amendment, a member of Congress named Edith Green said pithily, "It has been said that if this amendment is passed it will create profound social changes. May I say to you, it is high time some profound social changes were made in our society." Once we were grateful for those Molly Pitcher coloring books. We were grateful to have the access and stature once granted only to men. Forget gratitude. Given the complexity and richness of the lives many women have now cobbled out of past imperatives and present opportunities, real transformation will come when men live more like us.

Barbie at 35

SEPTEMBER 1994

MY THEORY IS THAT TO GET RID OF BARBIE you'd have to drive a silver stake through her plastic heart. Or a silver lamé stake, the sort of thing that might accompany Barbie's dream tent.

This is not simply because the original Barbie, launched lo these thirty-five years ago, was more than a little vampiric in appearance, more Natasha of *The Rocky and Bullwinkle Show* than the "ultimate girl next door" Mattel describes in her press kit.

It's not only that Barbie, like Dracula, can appear in guises that mask her essential nature: surgeon, astronaut, UNICEF ambassador. Nor that she is untouched by time, still the same parody of the female form she's been since 1959. She's said by her manufacturers to be "eleven and one-half stylish inches" tall. If she were a real live woman she would not have enough body fat to menstruate regularly. Which may be why there's no PMS Barbie.

The silver stake is necessary because Barbie—the issue, not the doll—simply will not be put to rest.

"Mama, why can't I have Barbie?"

"Because I hate Barbie. She gives little girls the message that the only thing that's important is being tall and thin and having a big chest and lots of clothes. She's a terrible role model."

"Oh, Mama, don't be silly. She's just a toy."

It's an excellent comeback; if only it were accurate. But consider the recent study at the University of Arizona investigating the attitudes of white and black teenage girls toward body image.

The attitudes of the white girls were a nightmare. Ninety percent expressed dissatisfaction with their own bodies, and many said they saw dieting as a kind of all-purpose panacea. "I think the reason I would diet would be to gain self-confidence," said one. "I'd feel like it was a way of getting control," said another.

And they were curiously united in their description of the perfect girl. She is five feet seven inches, weighs just over one hundred pounds, has long legs and flowing hair. The researchers concluded: "The ideal girl was a living manifestation of the Barbie doll."

While the white girls described an impossible ideal, black teenagers talked about appearance in terms of style, attitude, pride, and personality. White respondents talked thin, black ones shapely. Seventy percent of the black teenagers said they were satisfied with their weight, and there was little emphasis on dieting. "We're all brought up and taught to be realistic about life," said one, "and we don't look at things the way you want them to be. You look at them the way they are."

There's a quiet irony in that. While black women correctly complain that they are not sufficiently represented in advertisements, commercials, movies, even dolls, perhaps the scarcity of those idealized and unrealistic models may help to liberate black teenagers from ridiculous standards of appearance. When the black teenagers were asked about the ideal woman, many replied: Whose ideal? The perfect girl projected by the white world simply didn't apply to them or their community, which set beauty standards from within. "White girls," one black participant in the Arizona study wrote, "have to look like Barbie dolls."

There are lots of reasons teenage girls have such a distorted fun-house mirror image of their own bodies, so distorted that one study found that 83 percent wanted to lose weight, although 62 percent were in the normal range. Fashion designers still showcase anorexia chic; last year the supermodel Kate Moss was reduced to publicly insisting that, yes, she did indeed eat.

But long before Kate and Ultra Slim Fast came along, hanging over the lives of every little girl born in the second half of the twentieth century was the impossibly curvy shadow (40-18-32 in real-life terms) of Barbie. That preposterous physique, we learn as kids, is what a woman looks like with her clothes off. "Two Barbie dolls are sold every second," says Barbie's résumé, which is more extensive than that of Hillary Rodham Clinton. "Barbie doll has had more than a billion pairs of shoes . . . has had over 500 professional makeovers . . . has become the most popular toy ever created."

Has been single-handedly responsible for the popularity of silicone implants?

Maybe, as my daughter suggests while she whines in her Barbie-free zone, that's too much weight to put on something that's just a toy. Maybe not. Happy Birthday, Babs. Have a piece of cake. Have two.

Say Farewell to Pin Curls

MAY 2003

THIS BALMY STRETCH FROM EASTER until the end of school in June always reminds me of my mother messing around with my hair. Too often the kitchen smelled like the wallpaper was being chemically removed because of the fumes from Tonette, the home permanent for little girls. Afterward my head looked perpetually surprised. The thick straight bangs belied the ebullient frizz on either side, so that my face was a window with a flat shade and ruffled café curtains. We all had bangs then, so that our hair would not be in our faces, a habitual complaint by the mothers and the nuns. When my hair was in my face my mother referred to me as Veronica Lake.

Easter, May procession, class pictures, graduation. Pin curls, braids, ribbons, rollers. There exists not a single photo of significance from my childhood that shows my head as it was in nature. Occasionally the day was warm or wet enough to cause the phony curl to release before afternoon's end. This is why I look more or less normal in First Communion photographs, except for the veil and the hands prayerfully folded. Sitting here today I can re-create in my mind the sensation of bobby pins poking my scalp, the way sleeping on rollers feels like having a shoe box for a pillow. We were groomed then like baby beauty queens.

This is no longer my life, not as a person, not as a parent. I messed with my children's hair only when they were babies, to cut the boys' curls—they cried, I cried—and to secure the weirdly overweening topknot my daughter had for her first year. Still reeling from the counterculture internecine warfare of the late 1960s, I made a deal with myself: no fighting over clothes and hair. (I reserve the right to go ballistic about tats and piercings.) "My hair like Jesus wore it / Hallelujah I adore it / Hallelujah Mary loved her son / Why don't my mother love me?" That was the title song from the first rock musical, and the question of the time. Fathers threatened to throw sons with ponytails out of the house. What was the point of that?

It is one measure of the loosey-goosey child-rearing with which our parents sometimes reproach us—"I always let my babies cry themselves to sleep!"—that we have eliminated the barbershop as a battleground. In this way I have acquired a son with a Mohawk. I do not like this, although apparently everyone else finds it flattering. Some middle school boys even wrote a song about it. He has agreed to buzz it back into a more conventional hairstyle in time for the prom.

The prom was the last time I remember letting my mother mess around with my hair. She created a braided bun woven with costume jewelry pearls and was moved to tears by her skill and my altered appearance. I was luckier than those of my classmates who'd gone to the beauty parlor and came out with immense helmet hair-undos, looking like a cross between the bride and her own grandmother. For graduation my hair hung naturally, long and straight, in my face as I stepped to the podium. I cut it all off three weeks after my mother died, an act not of fashion but of self-abnegation. For a time all my brothers had hair longer than mine. It drove our father nuts.

It occurred to me, looking at Mohawk man and his equally unfettered siblings—two atheists, two vegetarians, three writers, three actors, one jock, and all in just three humans!—that there was a sad point to all that sectioning and spraying my mother did. She was trying to ease me, from the head down, into a life of masquerade. A quiet soul who had somehow found herself with a daughter so extroverted that it could be counted as a clinical diagnosis, she must have understood that conformity was my inevitable uncomfortable fate. The conventions of so-called femininity were every bit as rigid, as painful, and as false as those manic ringlets that made a brave show until they fell of their own weight. My mother could not have envisioned a future free of girdles and garter belts, deference and duty, permanent waves and teasing combs, a future of freedom. But that future was foretold in those boys who let their hair fall to their shoulders, the world according to the Kinks: "Girls will be boys and boys will be girls, it's a mixed up muddled up shook up world."

I don't know that it's necessarily easier to take freedom as your birthright, to think if someone looks twice at the cockscomb of hair sprouting above the shaved sides that it's their problem, dude. There are still standards. They are simply looser ones. And there's a tyranny of freedom, too, so that nonconformist becomes the new conformity. But I think this is the better way; a tie, it has always seemed to me, is nothing but a noose with a pleasing pattern. My daughter and her girlfriends all have this trick of making an impromptu bun with their long hair, quick as a wink, and it looks beautiful and unstudied (unsprayed!) and not at all as though they are trying to be miniature adults, which is how I look in so many of those pictures. My boys do their own buzz cuts with clippers they keep in the bathroom. The irony is that I wish they'd let their hair grow longer. But I try to keep my mouth shut. The hair wars, thank God, are over.

Our Radical, Ourselves

OCTOBER 1993

THE SMART SCHOLARSHIP GIRL from a sheltered environment whose self-image goes south in the polyglot and high-pressure world of college is a staple, of modern fiction and of life. I know her. I was she.

And that is why I recognized Katherine Ann Power when she turned herself in and was sent to jail, understood how it was possible in four years to go from the valedictorian of a Catholic girls' school to a campus radical who drove the getaway car in a 1970 bank robbery.

Some of us in our forties have to strain to remember the self we were years ago—the convictions, the ideals, the sex, the drugs, even some of the rock and roll. Good things grew in that environment: a healthy skepticism about foreign wars and government pronouncements, the erosion of authoritarianism in institutions and in family life as well.

But in retrospect so much of it was facile flash, posturing as politics. Onetime antiwar demonstrators acquired mortgages and slid quietly into neoconservatism. Jane Fonda's name became synonymous with aerobic exercise. Jerry Rubin went into networking and Bobby Seale into barbecue.

Katherine Power's life on the lam was almost a parody of how the fire-in-the-belly sixties transmogrified into the home-and-hearth cocooning of the nineties. She taught cooking classes, brought polenta to potluck suppers, jogged. She came in from the cold after she went into therapy.

It was a classist movement, the campus antiwar movement, and it was classist all over again as magazines and newspapers waxed poetic about the pain of Katherine Ann Power, surrendering after a lifetime on the run.

And then last week a woman stood up in a courtroom in Boston and provided a reality check. The oldest child in a large Catholic family—I recognized her, too. I could almost see her in her uniform when they came to the school, a school probably not much different from the one Katherine Ann Power attended, to deliver the bad news. Her name was Clare Schroeder, and her father, Walter, was the cop who was shot in the back during the bank robbery, the year Clare was seventeen.

Sergeant Schroeder, now a police officer herself, had come to Katherine Power's sentencing to bear witness to the victim, the kind of working man who was as strange to campus activism as a wingtip shoe, the kind once called a pig.

"The press and the public seem far more interested in the difficulties that Katherine Power has inflicted upon herself than in the very real and horrible suffering she inflicted upon my family," she said.

Katherine Power's social conscience was not transitory; when she sold her interest in an Oregon restaurant, she gave the money to a charity that fights world hunger, just as she had planned to give the money away after the bank robbery. She was confused and unhappy at college, her therapist has said, with a powerful yen to improve the world.

Had she been born ten years later, the valedictorian of Marycrest High School, once transplanted to Brandeis, might have joined a cult, or become bulimic, or tutored poor kids, or worked at a soup kitchen. But hers were more incendiary times, and instead there was Walter Schroeder, his widow, nine children without a father.

Oh, do I recognize Katherine Power. She is the embodiment of the chasm between the sixties and the nineties, like someone with a multiple personality disorder. It is almost as though a different Kathy drove three ex-cons and her roommate to the scene of the crime. The other personalities, the cook, the mother, the middle-aged woman, perhaps feel as if they scarcely know her, as we scarcely know our younger selves.

But our sympathy has to be for the family of Walter Schroeder, dead these twenty-three years. His daughter remembered how she once saw a picture of him in the paper, giving a child CPR, and how, at her father's wake, a woman introduced herself as that child's mother.

I know the importance of that now—the child, the mother, the man. There are many things to contemplate in the odyssey of Katherine Power. But the most important is this: A man died; his wife was left alone; his children grew up without him. If the last twenty-three years have given us a sense of proportion, then surely we all understand that they are the point of the story.

An Era Ends

MAY 1994

THERE WERE TWO PEOPLE IN THE BACK of the open limousine, a man and a woman, and then there was a muffled sound like firecrackers and the man slumped. And she came out of her seat and onto the back of the car, on her hands, on her knees, on some desperate journey never fully understood, and on film she did it again and again and again, through the decades, until you could close your eyes and see her, on her hands, on her knees.

Later, on the plane, when she stood next to the man who would take her husband's place, who would take the house where she had lived with her children, there was blood on the skirt of her suit, red faded to brown on pink. Her husband had symbolized hope and vigor, and his death seemed like the end of an era. But the era truly ended Thursday when she died, the embodiment of survival.

The moment when she crawled out onto the back of the open limousine in which her husband had been murdered was the first and last time the American people would see Jacqueline Bouvier

Kennedy Onassis crawl. In a time when the star-maker machinery would chew up, swallow, and spit out celebrity, she was the last great private public figure in this country. In a time of gilt and glitz and perpetual revelation, she was perpetually associated with that thing so difficult to describe yet so simple to recognize, the apotheosis of dignity.

Three decades ago that quality might have been laid at the door of a privileged upbringing, the best schools, couture clothes. But in the years since it has become clear that the rich may be different from you and me, but they are every bit as apt to be ill-mannered and stupid. Mrs. Onassis's dignity was a function of character, not money.

But neither privacy nor dignity is essentially lovable, so the explanation for why so many felt so saddened by the death of a woman they had never met or seen or even heard speak must lie elsewhere. Perhaps it lies, in some small fashion, in the immutability of her handsome face and lithe figure, so inimical to mortal illness. Several weeks ago an acquaintance said that she had lost her hair because of chemotherapy, and it was a little like being told that the earth was flat.

Perhaps people admired the life she had gone on to lead, the life that many other women of her generation embraced after the rules about what was wanted of women changed in the midstream of their lives. Serial lives: an accomplished hostess in the White House at the laughably young age of thirty-one, a book editor in New York at forty-five. Above all, a devoted mother. If we are judged by our works, then Mrs. Onassis must be remembered first for raising two children who, by all reports and against the considerable odds of public life, are fine people.

Perhaps part of the sadness is the resurrection of buried memories: the memory of the car, the suit, the devastated face imperfectly hidden by the black scrim of her funeral veil. A miscarriage, a stillborn child, another baby who died less than two days after birth. A marriage whose shortcomings she knew long before they were revealed to us.

The backseat of a limousine, empty except for a ceremonial bouquet of roses speckled with blood. My mother bought a pink bouclé suit with navy blue piping for Easter in 1963, and after November she never wore it again. It hung in the back of her closet, empty as an abandoned house.

This private woman known to all the world by her first name, who had been given so many advantages, earned something during those gray days: the right to be left alone, to do what she pleased, to have a long and happy life. She made all of that happen, except for longevity. It seemed an affront when photographers gathered for a shot of the body being taken from the building on Fifth Avenue. So many times photographed without raising a hand to shield her unreadable face. Leave her in peace.

She put a plaque in the Lincoln bedroom many years ago, as though to make the evanescent real: "In this room lived John Fitzgerald Kennedy with his wife, Jacqueline, during the 2 years, 10 months, and 2 days he was president of the United States— Jan. 20, 1961–Nov. 22, 1963." Mrs. Nixon had it taken down. But always there was this one person, with her world-famous face and her flawless posture, the last vestige of a charmed life that seemed to envelop us all for a time and then broke to bits, leaving her to pick up the pieces. Now even she is gone.

And Now for a Hot Flash

JULY 2002

WANT TO CLEAR A CROWDED ROOM? Try starting a discussion about menopause. I know; I did it several times before I got the message to sit down and shut up. Or, as one friend finally leaned in at lunch to say, sotto voce, "Just take the Premarin."

Now the whole world knows that that mantra simply will not do. Since the news broke of a government study showing that hormone replacement therapy does more harm than good, there's been discussion aplenty. Will those women who took hormones find other remedies? Will they stick with the combination of estrogen and progestin that the women in a federal test were urged to abandon? Will they sell their stock in Wyeth, the drug company whose shares tumbled on the news that their biggest-selling product might cause breast cancer, heart attack, and stroke?

But if the discussion merely concerns menopause and hormones, it will have been a huge missed opportunity. Instead this is the ideal time to confront the issue of one-size-fits-all health care, which has been the standard for far too long.

Here is where the expected attack on the medical establishment would normally begin. Not this time. As an editor once told me, "Cherchez le contract." By deciding to willy-nilly prescribe hormones to every female patient, from those who had dry skin to those tormented by hot flashes from hell, doctors were just doing what was easiest. By deciding to sell that medication by overstating its benefits and understating its risks, pharmaceutical companies were just doing what was most profitable.

Both groups are culpable, but so are patients, who need to take responsibility for their decisions, or for deciding not to decide and letting doctors and the marketplace decide for them. The case of hormone therapy is particularly glaring in this regard. How is it that the most ostentatiously self-aware generation of women in the history of this country allowed themselves to be led like lemmings to a "cure" for a condition that is not a disease and a "remedy" for symptoms that were originally described largely in terms of how they inconvenienced men?

That is how hormone therapy was first foisted wholesale on American females. A doctor whose own son says he was in the tank for the estrogen industry wrote a book called *Feminine Forever* about alleviating the symptoms of menopause. But many of the symptoms described in his book tended to fall into the "criticizes the way I chew and doesn't fix up her hair" school of husbandry.

Nevertheless, within a decade millions of women were taking hormones as a matter of course, even as one study after another emerged suggesting links with various cancers. Everybody did it, just like everybody with reproductive difficulties had hysterectomies and everybody with breast cancer had mastectomies.

Some of this treatment was appropriate and helpful; some was unnecessary and even harmful.

Doctors got a lot of the blame, and patients were portrayed as a victim class. That has become ridiculous. Publishing houses keep churning out more and more books on health. Newspapers and magazines run stories constantly. Holistic medicine and herbal remedies are finally getting the respect and attention they deserve. The Internet is not just a shopping channel for linens and things, but a boundless source of information on issues from nutrition to transplant surgery. When you type in the key words "hormone replacement therapy," you get almost 100,000 hits.

Fifty years ago a doctor said to my mother, in effect, "Just take the DES." Probably he didn't even name the stuff, just prescribed it, in a case that has become the poster child for bad medicine. DES is a synthetic estrogen that was said to prevent miscarriage, but didn't. What it did was cause cancer, infertility, and perhaps autoimmune problems in the daughters of those women who took it. As a result of my in utero DES exposure, the product of my mother's well-meaning ingestion of a hormone that her doctor automatically prescribed, I look at a prescription the way some people look at a loaded gun.

But rationally I also learned to bring the same set of questions I bring to my work to my health: What is this? Why is it necessary? What are the downsides? Where do I go for another opinion? In the drama of my body, I have become both the story and the reporter.

It is easier to simply take the pill, whatever it is, instead of studying up on diet, exercise, alternatives, the risk-benefit equation of surgery or drugs. What an orderly world it would be if the pill always did what it ought to, with no ill effects, no downside. But that's sci-fi, not reality. "I understand that medicine is not an exact science," it says on one surgical consent form. Where does that admission leave us? With choices, preferably informed ones, not the "yes, doctor" of years past. The day of the MDeity should be over; physicians have acted like little gods because patients have treated them as though they were. The woman who looks to a doctor to dictate rather than advise may wind up with treatment that she lives to regret. Or perhaps doesn't.

Sexual Assault,
Film at Eleven

JULY 2000

THIS TIME WE GOT TO SEE IT.

And seeing it was not pretty, at least unless you were as twisted as the men captured on the videotapes. They were on the hunt in Central Park, and their prey was female: women crying, women screaming, women with their arms crossed over their denuded chests so they would not be as exposed as they felt. They were the prey, but it was the men who behaved like animals.

Exactly how many women were sexually abused by a mob in the wake of the annual Puerto Rican Day parade is still unsure; at last count, it was around fifty. But some of the amateur videotapes examined by prosecutors show women groped and stripped and molested who have not yet come forward. Some of those who have been questioned have testified to "digital penetration," a clinical term that makes your skin crawl and your stomach roil. "Get them!" the men shouted as they chased their victims down the park pathways and surrounded them with a ring of inexorable hands. "Get the bitches!"

What happened after the parade happens in this country, in every country, every day. Oh, it doesn't often happen in broad daylight, and the numbers are not usually so huge, except in war zones: dozens of predatory assailants, dozens of weeping women. And we don't usually have film to testify to what actually happened.

But this turning women into meat puppets is as common as rain. Never mind the effects of Jerry Springer or MTV. That is sand upon bedrock, and the bedrock is this: that there are still many many men who feel, deep inside, that women as a group are just something—not someone, something—to be used and humiliated. They grope on the subway; they beat up at home. They rape and sodomize, male against female, the world's oldest bias crime.

"Welcome back to the caveman times!" you can hear one of the guys yelling hoarsely as a woman runs by clutching her torn shirt.

Caveman times and medieval times and Victorian times and war times and peace times. To suggest that this is a product of our times is an excuse for behavior as old as time. There's no evidence that there were fewer sexual assaults in olden days when a glimpse of stocking was said to be something shocking; there's only evidence that it was secret then, that no one told.

While Mayor Giuliani's first response to the park rampage was to talk about how crime in New York was down, rape has not decreased markedly in the way other violent crimes have. And while Central Park is safer than it has been in years, it is dotted with green and quiet places where some of the bloodiest sexual assaults in recent years have taken place: the lawn where Robert Chambers left Jennifer Levin's body, the place where the Central Park jogger lay unconscious after being gang-raped, the area where a Brazilian runner was murdered by a still unknown assailant.

But there is no point in picking on the park. There was also the basement in a New Jersey suburb where a group of popular high school boys molested a retarded girl, the pool table in a Rhode Island port town where a group of working men took turns raping a woman one night. Dorm rooms and bleachers. Kosovo and Johannesburg. White, black, professional men, habitual convicts, well-spoken, crude, strangers, acquaintances, even friends. Read the case files and they are all there, sharing some peculiar sense of violent entitlement.

Over the centuries the excuses for this have been many and various: She was a servant, a slave, a prostitute, an infidel, a wife. A century ago sexual assault was explained as the inevitable explosive acting-out of men in a repressive atmosphere; now it is supposed to be the inevitable effect of a permissive environment. When we natter on about our culture, about how this is a corollary of violent lyrics and explicit movies, it is no more than a different kind of excuse. It is not entirely their fault; rap music made them do it, or halter tops.

Nonsense. When skirts were longer and necklines higher, certain men were still holding women down and forcing themselves upon them in an age-old act of power and dominance. And humiliation, of course: The men on the videotape laugh while the women weep and scream. There is no mystery about whether this is wrong. The difference between the woman in a wet T-shirt contest and the woman with the wet T-shirt being ripped from her body as she pleads for mercy, for respect, for humanity, can be contained in a single word. That word is *consent*. Why is it so simple for some boys to learn they cannot lift a person's wallet and yet so difficult for them to understand they cannot lift a person's skirt?

There is only one good thing about what happened in Central Park, and that is that we saw. This comes at a cost; what was the deal, really, with the guys with the video cameras, many of whom seem as though they were producing amateur bachelor party films for the emotionally stunted instead of creating evidence of a crime? But at least what is on film cannot be minimized or denied. "This is not a crime that occurs in broad daylight with many witnesses," wrote Linda Fairstein in her book *Sexual Violence.* But Ms. Fairstein, who runs the Sex Crimes Prosecution Unit of the Manhattan DA's office, has seen it all in her line of work—a defense attorney who once held up a pair of leopard panties during his summation to prove that an investment banker was asking for it, a rapist who came back to the restroom stall where his victim still cowered because he had put down his newspaper during the act and wanted to retrieve it. Now she is overseeing a broad-daylight case, with a VCR as both investigator and witness. That is new. All the rest of this horrid spectacle is as old as Earth.

And Now, Babe Feminism

JANUARY 1994

WHEN YOU DON'T WANT TO WRITE about something as badly as I don't want to write about the Bobbitt case, it's nature's way of telling you to figure out why. Too easy to say that there's nothing more to say. Not good enough to note that the case of the woman who cut off her husband's penis has evoked more bad double entendres than anything in recent memory.

No, none of that is why I've avoided the Bobbitts. It's because of feminism. It's because, three decades after the movement for women's equality began, the Bobbitt case is what naysayers truly believe it is all about: cutting it off.

But never fear, gentlemen; castration was really not the point of feminism, and we women are too busy eviscerating one another to take you on. Witness an article in *Esquire* magazine about a group of young women characterized as "do me feminists" because of an agenda heavy on sex when and how they want it, with no guilt, no regrets. One of them even shows up for an interview with a consensual spanking video called *Blame It on Bambi*.

While the feminist theorists Catharine MacKinnon and Andrea Dworkin normally get slammed for their views on pornography, in the *Esquire* article one is trashed for her lack of sex appeal and the other for her heft. It's a little like turnabout on the bad old "Can a feminist wear mascara?" days when Gloria Steinem's politics were overshadowed by her streaked hair. It's certainly just as stupid.

"A lot of us just want to go spray-paint and make out with our boyfriends and not worry about oppression," Lois Maffeo, twenty-nine, a singer, says in *Esquire.* Cool—that'll make it a lot easier when you get a straight job and get paid a whole lot less than the guy you work next to.

Men who have grown tired of complaints about equal pay and violence against women will find the ideas here more cheering, especially the idea that Good Feminism = Great Sex. And anyone who has been suspicious of the movement heretofore can have his fears confirmed: We're angry because we're ugly.

"There are a lot of homely women in women's studies," Christina Hoff Sommers, a professor at Clark University in Massachusetts, is quoted as saying. "Preaching these anti-male, anti-sex sermons is a way for them to compensate for various heartaches—they're just mad at the beautiful girls." Nonsense. Professor Sommers might not be doing what she's doing today if many women, some attractive, some not, had not fomented social change over the last three decades because of much more than heartaches.

That change is far from over; there's still plenty to do, and much of it will be working with our male friends. But seeing sexual aggression as the solution is as reductive as seeing pornography as the problem. And it has precious little to do with much of real life, with raising children, making a living, or learning about yourself.

It's babe feminism—we're young, we're fun, we do what we want in bed—and it has a shorter shelf life than the feminism of sisterhood. I've been a babe, and I've been a sister. Sister lasts longer. In her new book, *Fire with Fire,* the feminist Naomi Wolf writes, "The male body is home to me." I like guys, but my own body is home to me. That was the point of feminism: I got custody of myself.

Esquire also published a survey of one thousand young women in this issue. Asked if they'd rather be brilliant but plain or sexy but dumb, 74 percent went for brains. (Maybe they'll all teach women's studies.) While a do me feminist editor was describing proactive sex—"pretend you're a burglar and you've broken in here . . ."—the women in the poll were asked to choose between hugging without sex and sex without hugging. Hugging won by a landslide.

And 65 percent of the respondents said they'd rather win the Pulitzer Prize than be Miss America. That's far more representative of what the women's movement has done than Lorena Bobbitt's do-it-yourself surgery or somebody's in-your-face burglary/bustier fantasies.

Because it's important to remember that feminism is no longer a group of organizations or leaders. It's the expectations that parents have for their daughters, and their sons, too. It's the way we talk about and treat one another. It's who makes the money and who makes the compromises and who makes the dinner. It's a state of mind. It's the way we live now. Our Bambi, ourselves? Oh, please.

Uncle Sam and
Aunt Samantha

NOVEMBER 2001

ONE OUT OF EVERY FIVE NEW RECRUITS in the United States military is female.

The Marines gave the Combat Action Ribbon for service in the Persian Gulf to twenty-three women.

Two female soldiers were killed in the bombing of the USS *Cole.*

The Selective Service registers for the draft all male citizens between the ages of eighteen and twenty-five.

What's wrong with this picture?

As Americans read and realize that the lives of most women in this country are as different from those of Afghan women as a Cunard cruise is from maximum security lockdown, there's nonetheless been little attention paid to one persistent gender inequity in U.S. public policy. An astonishing anachronism, really: While women are represented today in virtually all fields, including the armed forces, only men are required to register for the military draft that would be used in the event of a national security crisis.

Since the nation is as close to such a crisis as it's been in more than sixty years, it's a good moment to consider how the draft wound up in this particular time warp. It's not the time warp of the Taliban, certainly, stuck in the worst part of the thirteenth century, forbidding women to attend school or hold jobs or even reveal their arms, forcing them into sex and marriage. Our own time warp is several decades old. The last time the draft was considered seriously was twenty years ago, when registration with the Selective Service was restored by Jimmy Carter after the Soviet invasion of—déjà vu alert!—Afghanistan. The president, as well as the army chief of staff, asked at the time for the registration of women as well as men.

Amid a welter of arguments—women interfere with esprit de corps, women don't have the physical strength, women prisoners could be sexually assaulted, women soldiers would distract male soldiers from their mission—Congress shot down the notion of gender-blind registration. So did the Supreme Court, ruling that since women were forbidden to serve in combat positions and the purpose of the draft was to create a combat-ready force, it made sense not to register them.

But that was then, and this is now. Women have indeed served in combat positions, in the Balkans and the Middle East. More than forty thousand managed to serve in the Persian Gulf without destroying unit cohesion or failing because of upper body strength. Some are even now taking out targets in Afghanistan from fighter jets, and apparently without any male soldier falling prey to some predicted excess of chivalry or lust.

Talk about cognitive dissonance. All these military personnel, male and female alike, have come of age at a time when a significant level of parity was taken for granted. Yet they are supposed to accept that only males will be required to defend their country in a time of national emergency. This is insulting to men. And it is insulting to women. Caroline Forell, an expert on women's legal rights and a professor at the University of Oregon, puts it bluntly: "Failing to require this of women makes us lesser citizens."

Neither the left nor the right has been particularly inclined to consider this issue judiciously. Many feminists came from the antiwar movement and have let their distaste for the military in general and the draft in particular mute their response. In 1980 NOW released a resolution that buried support for the registration of women beneath opposition to the draft, despite the fact that the draft had been redesigned to eliminate the vexing inequities of Vietnam, when the sons of the working class served and the sons of the Ivy League did not. Conservatives, meanwhile, used an equal-opportunity draft as the linchpin of opposition to the equal rights amendment, along with the terrifying specter of unisex bathrooms. (I have seen the urinal, and it is benign.) The legislative director of the right-wing group Concerned Women for America once defended the existing regulations by saying that most women "don't want to be included in the draft." All those young men who went to Canada during Vietnam and those who today register with fear and trembling in the face of the Trade Center devastation might be amazed to discover that lack of desire is an affirmative defense.

Parents face a series of unique new challenges in this more egalitarian world, not the least of which would be sending a daughter off to war. But parents all over this country are doing that right now, with daughters who enlisted; some have even expressed surprise that young women, in this day and age, are not required to register alongside their brothers and friends. While all involved in this debate over the years have invoked the assumed opposition of the people, even ten years ago more than half of all Americans polled believed women should be made eligible for the draft. Besides, this is not about comfort but about fairness. My son has to register with the Selective Service this year, and if his sister does not when she turns eighteen it makes a mockery, not only of the standards of this household, but of the standards of this nation.

It is possible in Afghanistan for women to be treated like little more than fecund pack animals precisely because gender fear and ignorance and hatred have been codified and permitted to hold sway. In this country, largely because of the concerted efforts of those allied with the women's movement over a century of struggle, much of that bigotry has been beaten back, even buried. Yet in improbable places the creaky old ways surface, the ways that suggested we women were made of finer stuff. The finer stuff was usually porcelain, decorative, and on the shelf, suitable for meals and show. Happily, the finer stuff has been transmuted into the right stuff. But with rights come responsibilities, as teachers like to tell their students. This is a responsibility that should fall equally upon all, male and female alike. If the empirical evidence is considered rationally, if the decision is divested of outmoded stereotypes, that's the only possible conclusion to be reached.

The Lone Pilgrim

FEBRUARY 1993

THE OTHER NIGHT I READ FROM HER WORK at a memorial service for the writer Laurie Colwin, whom I met only once but admired enormously. The essay, "Alone in the Kitchen with an Eggplant," has always seemed particularly evocative of the way young single women live in New York City, where Laurie lived and, incredibly, died at age forty-eight.

It is about entertaining in an extremely small apartment. "Naturally, there being no kitchen, there was no kitchen sink," she wrote. "I did the dishes in a plastic pan in the bathtub and set the dish drainer over the toilet."

This is how real life began for many of us, in a closet of a place with a handful of recipes for things like spaghetti carbonara and chicken chasseur. There followed the convertible couches and flea-market antiques, a place with dining room and dishwasher, the good butcher, the nice preschool.

It had somehow not occurred to me that next would be the perfect memorial service.

Not because I had never felt the hot breath of nevermore on my neck. That is always part of it, your own mortality, every time someone tells you of a friend of a friend with breast cancer or AIDS. It took little imagination the other night to squint at the black surround of the stage and the spot-lit podium and imagine someone, somewhere, remembering me.

And I could only hope that I would be valued half as well as Laurie Colwin was by her friends, acquaintances, and readers. The writer Walter Abish saying: "Laurie enhanced. It's as simple as that." Scott Spencer talking of how she shopped his first manuscript around town, pretending to be an agent, adding, "She saw me in ways I had never seen myself before and never since."

Laurie Colwin was a splendid writer, her characters wrought with perfect pitch, her worldview sharp and telling but neither dark nor mean. I was always cheered by the fact that it was possible for a modern writer to believe in family, to believe in love, to audaciously title one novel *Happy All the Time,* and yet to tell the indisputable truth in her fiction at a time when truth telling was assumed to consist of nihilism and negativity.

And I always thought of her as the prototype of my people: one of the young women who came to the city to make a reputation and stayed to build a family and a life. If you drew a map of the connections among those of us who fit into that category, at the magazines and newspapers and publishing houses, it would look like a gargantuan spiderweb.

It was not that we necessarily knew one another, but that we knew of one another's lives, in the manner of a small town. In fact our lives were captured in Laurie Colwin's work, from the teeny-tiny apartments to the erudite, impossible love affairs to the edgy, loving marriages. Most of us had just managed to master family life; it seemed far too early for funerals at the churches where we once attended weddings.

I know this terrain. I have written black-bordered thank-you notes. But the death of my mother when I was nineteen was my great aberration, the thing that set me apart, and suddenly, the other evening, I realized that such memorial services would become our abominable commonplace, this thing that brought us together. Said Jonathan Yardley of *The Washington Post*, "Dear girl, dear friend, the world is too much smaller without you." Our circles will shrink. Mortality is a game of musical chairs.

It was the agony I apprehended when I was younger. It is the nullity that strikes me now, the simply not being there as the years go on, in the kitchen, the classroom, at the bus stop, like the dark area on an X-ray.

They played Sam and Dave before the memorial service began. There were lots of laughs, because Laurie was often a very funny writer, and lots of talk about food and friendship, because she was as good a cook as she was a friend, and her reputation for both was legendary.

The memorial service did what a memorial service is meant to do: It made the woman alive again, as though at any moment she would step from the wings, like the happy ending to a bad dream. Or show up in the empty chair in the second row, like one of those arch 1930s movies with a slightly see-through actress.

But in truth the chair was empty. At the end of "The Lone Pilgrim," one of her finest stories, she writes of how, in facing the forest of our future, we "strain through the darkness to see ahead." Ahead once seemed a very long way to see. Not anymore.

Say Good-bye
to the Virago

MAY 2003

HILLARY.

Now that I have your attention, here's the inside scoop on the book, from someone who hasn't read it yet but knows the subject: She worked hard, she did well, she had doubts, she made mistakes, she didn't know, she found out, she freaked out, she went on, she worked hard, she did well.

Yep, it's the story of Everywoman. And once again the former first lady, the junior senator from New York, the uberauthor, the lightning rod, will be held to account for Everywoman's compromises, changing roles, and inevitable shortcomings. Not to mention Everyone Else's discomfort with all of the above.

In the process the unremarkable will be made astonishing. The wife of a womanizer who didn't know and then forgave! The brilliant helpmate with her own ambitions! The public servant who wanted to make some big bucks from a book! Be still my heart! Television pundits suggested that her memoir is designed to abet Senator Clinton's push toward the presidency, as though writing a book was a nefarious plot to circumvent the usual sterling-silver process of phony ads and staged debates.

So let me get this straight: A former first lady wants to write a personal history that casts her in a positive light, just as virtually every first lady has done before her. And a woman who has given some of the best years of her life to public service when she could have been making a mint in the private sector, who has shown time and time again that she has a sophisticated grasp of national issues, who was overwhelmingly elected against all odds to the Senate, may want to run for president.

Where's the problem?

The most interesting development is that there isn't any problem, at least for many Americans. A Gallup poll last week in *USA Today* showed that almost two out of three considered Senator Clinton honest and trustworthy, as well as warm and friendly, while a whopping 93 percent think of her as intelligent. And a story in *The New York Times* last year quoted her astonished Republican Senate colleagues on how pleasant and collegial the artist formerly known as the virago of Pennsylvania Avenue was, once you got to know her.

"What a surprise, right?" the senator herself said with her piano-key smile at a charity event not long afterward.

Those still behind the curve on the demonization front fall largely into two groups: the right wing and the media. Maybe that's because Hillary has never fit easily into the boxes convention and custom create for women. She tacked on her husband's surname, and she messed around with her hair, but she couldn't hide the fact that she was smarter and more ambitious than most people. If she were male, both those qualities might have been seen as unremarkable. No excuse, just fact. Being called "opinionated" when we have opinions, "feisty" when we're angry, "bossy" when we're assertive. Deal with it. That's what Hillary has done, big-time.

Unlike Martha Stewart, the other smart blonde on the hot seat last week, Hillary didn't present a convincing facade. Note well that when Martha pretended to be all about gilding and forced bulbs, people loved her. When it became clear that behind the work shirt was a sharky corporate giant with a ruthless streak as wide as a banquet tablecloth, her approval ratings dropped. Now that she's been nailed to the wall by the feds (and always use a small piece of masking tape so the plaster won't shatter!), there's a sympathy vote. How well the damsel in distress still plays, even if she's accused of insider trading!

Even in distress Hillary has soldiered on, damned if she does and damned if she doesn't, like most powerful women, expected to be tough as nails and warm as toast both at the same time. (My favorite reflection of this is the *New Yorker* cartoon that shows a king and queen in the throne room, with the queen complaining, "Yes, but when a woman beheads someone they call her a bitch!") If she'd left Bill she would have been pilloried; she was pilloried when she stayed. If she'd failed to write about l'affaire Lewinsky, she would have been accused of shortchanging the reader and the publisher. Because she did, it is considered unseemly or political.

"I have created a lot of cognitive dissonance," she once said, and even in those who should know better. During a 1994 interview, I asked her skeptically about a much-publicized trip she'd made to a Safeway. Weren't the pink sweater and the chat with the produce manager merely a cover-up for a very different sort of woman?

She leaned forward and asked what I had done that morning and what I planned to do that night. Hadn't I taken my kids to

school? Wasn't I planning to cook dinner? Was that domestic behavior merely a cover-up for the liberal feminist columnist lurking beneath the surface?

I learned two things that day: not to apply standards to the
lives of others that I wouldn't want applied to my own, and not to
underestimate Hillary Rodham Clinton. Those two lessons go on
sale in bookstores across America this week.

Not a Womb
in the House

NOVEMBER 2003

SOMETIMES THE PICTURES DO TELL THE STORY. There was
a raft of wire-service photographs of invited guests saluting the
president as he signed a bill banning a late-abortion procedure.
Not a working uterus in sight, not a person who could become
pregnant and be tortured and overwhelmed by the future. Orrin,
Rick, Jerry, Tommy, John: the functional equivalent of signing a
bill affecting black Americans amid self-congratulatory white
guys. Did no one notice the essential disconnect of having a
bunch of gray-haired men passing judgment on the bodily func-
tions of a nation's young women? Or was it just too tough to get
female leaders to show up for the celebration?

I am so tired of abortion. Discussions of it are the most mere-
tricious in modern public policy. Even as the president was vowing to sign a bill that would outlaw a procedure that accounts for
a handful of the terminations in America, he was opining that the
country was not yet ready to make abortion illegal. He was using

one hand to corral the right wing and the other to wave off the concerns of moderates. How dare the father of two daughters play politics with the womb?

I am so tired of abortion. Its opponents too often have a hidden agenda. Some of the men at that bill-signing support not only a ban on all abortions, but also the rolling back of other rights for the women of America. They are people who have indicated by word and deed that modern women have forgotten their proper place. They are clergy who have twisted the word of God to turn it into an instrument of gender bigotry. And they have clearly taken note of the fact that women who can control their fertility are more able to control their future.

But those of us who support legal abortion are not immune to criticism, particularly in the current debate over a procedure of half-delivering a fetus and crushing its skull, a procedure that has to repel and unnerve even the staunchest believer. Say what you will about the slippery antiabortion slope: This is not the place to ask Americans to make their stand on this issue. We can argue all we want that doctors should be able to make their own decisions about what procedure to use. We can argue all we want that this procedure is rare, and performed only under wrenching circumstances. But by seeming to lump these abortions with other, earlier ones, we have lost credibility. Because that is clearly not how reasonable people see this.

Abortion rights supporters have not kept pace with the technology. As sophisticated sonograms become more widely used, as it is possible to see the face of a fetus clearly, it will become ever more important to be painfully honest about what really happens here. Something dies when an abortion is performed. It is not yet a baby. It is not remotely anyone else's business. But something does die. In the tension between woman and fetus, the woman has the right to choose. But she cannot really choose to ignore that there are two important parts to this equation. Biology tells her so.

By contrast, abortion opponents have never understood the psychology. They do not understand that there are times when an embryo is an embedded blessing, and times when it is an incubus, a nightmare, a curse. They do not understand how deeply felt is the notion that the right to the processes of your own body is the great inviolate right. How can they? How can President Bush understand this issue when he stacks the seats with people who can never know what it feels like to be pregnant? Say this for President Clinton: When he vetoed this same bill, at his side were five women who had had late abortions and who testified to their feelings, their reasons, and their pain. How many ordinary women has George W. Bush ever heard discuss this matter? Why was his wife not by his side when he signed this bill, instead of Dennis Hastert and Cardinal Egan?

It is like so much else in public policy: deciding what to provide for the poor without speaking to poor people, deciding what to do for the citizens of other nations without having any idea what they want themselves. It is paternalistic and insulting. Like those photographs. How can those men sit and smile and clap their hands when somewhere a woman with a horribly deformed fetus may have to face a more difficult and perhaps disfiguring procedure if she cannot bear to wait until the end of its gestation to watch it die?

I am so tired of abortion; tired of the dishonesty of the arguments, of the intractability of the conflict, mainly of the insensibility of those who pass judgment. No matter what is legislated, adjudicated, or pontificated, women will continue to find a way to end pregnancies that they cannot bear to turn, by the hospitality of their own bodies, into children. They always have; they always will. Knitting needles, caustic chemicals, medical residents, un-licensed doctors, sympathetic nurses, bootleg curettes.

Let those old men try to comfort the parents and the children of those women after they are dead. Let them offer them their version of the words of God and see how much good they do. Let them say, "I understand." They will never understand.

4 Voice

THERE'S A SOUND THAT YOU CAN HEAR when an entire auditorium of people are following what you're saying from the stage. Or not a sound, exactly, but an atmosphere. It's what the soundman on a movie is after when he records what is called "room tone," a watchful waiting silence. It is what you have when you are telling a story at a dinner party and everyone is paying close attention, only bigger and better.

It is wonderful.

It doesn't happen all the time, obviously. Sometimes you can hear coughing and shifting and whispering and even the clarion call of a cell phone playing the opening notes of "Pomp and Circumstance" or "La Cucaracha." Sometimes you can feel that you've lost the alchemy, the dramatic tension, the tone, or the content that allows people to follow you from thought to thought to thought along the delicate rosary of theme. But when it comes together, the public conversation between one and hundreds, it can be an incandescent thing, part communication, part performance.

Public oratory has fallen out of fashion in the last century, although once it was a form of entertainment as well attended as the theater, or hangings. The presidential speech has become an exercise in safe sound bites; only Reagan's "morning in America" and Kennedy's "ask not what your country can do for you" have resonance, and no speech since the Gettysburg Address has survived in its entirety in the public mind. Candidates' speeches have become so anodyne, designed to mollify every conceivable group, that the verbs must be passive and the adverbs few and far between.

Public speaking is rarely taught in schools anywhere, and it's frequently cited by business types as the greatest anxiety associated with their work. It's so fraught under the best of circumstances—Are the acoustics decent? Will the mike work? Will some heckler or whacko disrupt the proceedings, or some boor talk all the way through?—that I can't imagine doing it unless you could do so without anxiety. It's never made me nervous. Part is just personality, extroversion marbled with bombast and unreasonable confidence. I am, after all, an oldest child. I practiced on a captive audience of four.

After a speech it's fairly common for listeners to remark, amazed, "You talk just like you write." That's no accident; for one thing, I work from a prepared text, so in some very real sense any speech I give is a piece of writing. I haven't reached the heights of extempore, inhabited, in my experience, by only three speakers I've ever heard, Hillary Rodham Clinton, Mario Cuomo, and Peter Gomes, the chaplain at Harvard. All three speak beautifully without any prepared text, but if their remarks are later transcribed, they indeed sound like a fully cogent essay. Which is some trick.

But a writer's voice, for those of us who speak in public, is a portmanteau, toted from one arena to another. I've always written by ear; I never hand in an essay, or even a book, without reading aloud to hear the clunks that need to be fixed. Ideally all of my written work should have some elements of an audiogram, picking up my particular syntax and turn of phrase. That's why there's a professor at Vassar who can figure out the author of various anonymous texts. To be a good writer, and a successful public speaker, the voice should be distinctive.

But I'm not sure the two forms are completely transferable. I'm always editing speeches as I give them, aware that the long baroque sentences that work when a reader is eyeballing them can leave me breathless at a podium, that some more formal locutions sound forced. And I'm always hoping that no one has already heard the cheerful anecdote or the slyly sexist joke. The Internet has made any hesitation about seeing the spoken word in print a bit vainglorious. Suddenly remarks at a commencement or a book festival will appear in the e-mail queues of thousands of strangers connected by friendship, family ties, or simply the forwarding lists of one or both of the above.

A reader will mention a piece you've written and you realize it was not a written piece at all but a spoken one, transcribed and let loose in cyberspace to be sent to one person who sent it to ten, ten who send it to a hundred, in a kind of communications pyramid scheme. People ask frequently if I give the same speech for every occasion. I rarely have, but the proliferation of words online makes it particularly chancy to do so today. What a shock for a listener, to realize you have taken as your text the self-same five thousand words passed along by a coworker just the day before. And when people ask for a copy of a particular speech, to show their daughter or their mother or merely to hold the moment and the message, I'm always keenly aware of a quote from a nineteenth-century British prime minister, a renowned orator himself: "Few speeches which have produced an electrical effect on an audience can bear the colourless photography of a printed record."

The Key to Success

OVER THE DESK IN MY HOME OFFICE, just above the telegram
I received in 1992 when I won the Pulitzer Prize, there are two
pieces of art. One is a framed photograph by Joyce Ravid of an
easel standing in one corner of what appears to be a hotel corri-
dor. On the easel is a placard that reads THE KEY TO SUCCESS: FOL-
LOW YOUR HEART.

The other is an original cartoon, the comic strip *Brenda Starr,
Reporter*. A friend runs to the desk of the ace newswoman, calling, "Brenda! Anna Quindlen just called! She said your story
was brilliant. She wondered if you'd like to quit the newspaper
and co-author a sensitive feminist novel with her."

I first wanted to be a reporter when I was a little girl because
of Brenda, because of her exotic travels, her exotic boyfriend,
above all her exotic fall of red hair, and it is still a bit difficult for
me to believe that I made a cameo appearance in her life. But
everything that happened to me after I announced that I was

trading one wonderful job for another has been difficult to fathom as well. Difficult to fathom, but illustrative, too, of what I once wanted, of what I now value, of what the world thinks we should ask of work and life.

For five years I had been an opinion columnist for *The New York Times*, perhaps the best and most desirable position in American journalism. I was the only woman in that job, and so I became the most visible woman for *Times* readers. Rumors flew that when my writing life was over I would help lead the paper for which I'd worked for almost twenty years.

But I'd led a triple life that, in some sense, was in opposition to that sort of future. While much of my time was spent in reporting and writing on the issues of the day, on abortion, health care, gay rights, and the political circus, some was spent creating a world out of whole cloth, writing novels, publishing two in five years. And while both of those jobs were extraordinarily time-consuming and mentally draining, my most difficult took place, not at the computer, but in the kitchen, where I was the more or less full-time mother of three young children.

If that sounds hectic, it was. Perhaps the best illustration of how wacky our house could be was the evening our second son, Christopher, came downstairs and said, "Some man just called but I told him you couldn't talk because you were making dinner." Next day I discovered the man was civil rights leader Jesse Jackson, who wanted to talk about the situation in Haiti.

In television sitcoms that sort of thing makes for great hilarity; in real life it brings burnout. Too many loves, too little time. So it happened that one day I was walking down a country road after having finished the first draft of a novel called *One True Thing* when I suddenly thought I would simply like to embrace the challenging and enormously satisfying job of writing fiction full-time. And over time I decided, as my new photograph says, to follow my heart, to trade in my opinion column and public notoriety and take a chance on a different sort of life.

Eudora Welty once wrote, "Novels and stories always will be put down little by little out of personal feeling and personal beliefs arrived at alone and at firsthand over a period of time as time is needed. To go outside and beat the drum is only to interrupt, interrupt, and so finally to forget and to lose. Fiction has, and must keep, a private address." The most public of women, whose readers knew more about her husband, her children, and her opinions than they did about those of many of their own friends, I decided the way to grow as a writer was to begin to keep a private address.

In May I told the publisher of the *Times*, who was keenly disappointed. And in September we told the rest of the world, who went a little nuts.

I'm not talking about the genuine regret many readers expressed about the end of our public conversations twice a week. That sentiment was, and still is, deeply gratifying. What's nicer than having people say they'll miss you when you're gone?

But that endearing regret was overshadowed by a great palpable incredulity, the sense that simply doing what you wanted was a bizarre and suspect course of action. What was the real story? my friends were asked. Had I been passed over for a top job, or was this merely a ploy, the professional version of playing hard to get? Yes, of course, I found fiction writing satisfying, they said dismissively. But was *satisfaction* (say that in tones of barely disguised contempt) enough to give up such a visible job for a nearly invisible one?

How to explain that reaction? I'm not sure I can. Is it a lingering Puritan ethic that posits that real work is arduous, onerous? Is it an investment in public life, in the household name and the magazine stories, that believes a private one is always less attractive? Of course, for many of us the question of doing what we want is a moot one: money comes between, the mortgage, the car payments, those day-to-day things that stand in the way of dreams. It's one reason I went into journalism in the first place; I was pretty sure, starting out, that I couldn't pay the rent writing fiction.

But the stories and opinion columns that charted my decision talked little of the book contract and working husband that had made my change of course possible. Most of them focused on what my decision said about women. Some said that my resignation proved that women couldn't really have it all. One ultraconservative wrote that it showed that women had no business in the workplace to begin with. An English professor in the Midwest said I was setting a bad example for younger women, who would think that they could follow me to home and hearth. (One thing I learned from the uproar is that almost no one considers fiction writing a real job, or, as a subway conductor asked me one morning, "How's retirement?") Everyone seemed to agree that one woman could be made to stand for all women, and that my decision said something monumental about feminism and the social changes of the last quarter century.

Well, maybe it did. The fallout certainly spoke to how little some of our attitudes have changed. Part of it had to do with the fact that I was the only female voice on the opinion page; if there had been two or three other women columnists, as there should be by any statistical demographic measure, there wouldn't have been half the fuss. And while our own story about my decision was headlined QUINDLEN LEAVING TIMES TO BE A FULL-TIME NOVELIST, most of the stories suggested that I wanted to spend more time with my family, ignoring the fact that I had worked at home and around my children's school schedules during my years as a columnist. Perhaps the sheer lunacy of giving up such an influential job could only be explained in terms of an estrogen surge, by the softer, more feminine (more emotional? more irrational?) side of my woman's character. In fact, maybe the good sense of it can only be explained by that side as well, the side that, despite all the speculation about a future in management, could never see holding a job that might mean I would get home from work hours after our kids got home from school. Maybe we women remain better able to make decisions based on the voice that speaks from our heart and not that great inchoate "they" out there that dictates career paths and life goals based on a cookie-cutter view of success and a disdain for personal happiness as an end in itself.

Although many women said they were disappointed to lose a public female voice, they seemed more open to the idea of having serial lives, of constant reinvention, of discarding one self and assuming another. Perhaps, too, women know they will be criticized no matter what choices they make: We know from experience of the mother working full-time taking care of her children who is ignored at parties because if she doesn't have a job title, she can't be interesting, or, conversely, of the mother with a job outside her home whose friends or relations imply that her children are being allowed to play barefoot in the snow.

The reaction to my decision reinforced a sense I had always had that for many women, life is a circle, for men a straight line. The guys seemed to have an idea of career that was inevitably a ladder. Some were unhappy about that; they would quietly confide that they, too, had always wanted to try another path but had somehow never gone ahead with it. Others were simply bemused and, often, dismissive of what I had done: Why in the world, many seemed to imply, would anyone pass on the chance to take the next rung? Or take a chance on a new incline that might not pay off as handsomely as the old familiar one? My decision proved what he'd always known, one corporate giant told a mutual friend: "Women are afraid of success."

I understand that straight-ahead definition of the good life, although it seems to me to have as much to do with a real and satisfying existence as my adolescent crushes had to do with real love. When I was nineteen years old, I watched my beloved mother die by inches of ovarian cancer, and after she had died, I was infected with a sense of drive and direction that catapulted me from one newspaper job to another in great haste.

By my early twenties I was already working at the *Times,* and over the next decade I moved from covering police and politics to a job writing a features column called "About New York." I was the first woman and the youngest person to do that column; I was also so ambitious that I once told a magazine writer that I intended to be childless all my life because I didn't want to trip over any little feet on my way to the top.

I am almost as incredulous, looking back at that young woman, as are many of those now observing her, in middle age, deciding to take a less spectacular path. To that extent my children were indeed behind this decision, as they have been behind literally every decision about the broad parameters of my life I have made since the eldest was born a dozen years ago. They have given me perspective, on the pursuit of joy and the passage of time. I miss too much when I am out of their orbit, and as they grow, like some time-lapse photograph that makes a flower out of a bud in scant minutes, I understand that I will have time to pursue a more frantic agenda when they have gone on to pursue their own. But they have made a more frantic agenda seem somehow less seductive than a satisfying one.

I once found in the keen sense of mortality I took from my mother's early death a belief that there was no time to stop an upward trajectory for even an instant. Today it means to me that the time we are afforded to find happiness and satisfaction cannot be spared or wasted, and that whenever possible dreams must be pursued, not deferred.

I have no fear of success. Perhaps I may never have it again on the scale I once did, where waiters recognized the name on my credit card and shoppers stopped me in the supermarket to tell me they loved my writing. Maybe I will miss my old work, so determined by the agitated pace of current events, will miss being a public voice for political concerns. I don't think so. I sink into this next new novel with a kind of surrender impossible before. Sink, too, into a more copacetic domestic routine. "You wind up making a lot of soup," said a friend who is working on a voluminous social history. She was right. Jesse Jackson no longer calls. The house smells like lentils. Imaginary people come to life beneath my fingers.

And I keep coming back to a song by Stephen Sondheim in his musical *Follies*. One of the characters, a terribly successful diplomat, sings bitterly of his missed opportunities: "You take one road / You try one door / There isn't time for any more / One's life consists of either-or / One has regrets / Which one forgets / And as the years go by / The road you didn't take hardly comes to mind, does it?"

Let others say what it all means; I'm not in that business anymore. But this I know: I am a very lucky woman.

The Story of Us

I WAS HAVING BREAKFAST WITH A FRIEND the other day, and I mentioned that I forget everything these days. I think the issue came up because I'd just forgotten the name of her teenage son, whom I've known since he was three. I didn't feel that bad, since that morning I'd forgotten my own home phone number.

And I didn't feel that bad because she's one of us. You know what I mean. All of us here today are one of us. We share many of the same great educational backgrounds and jobs, privileged existences and lucky children. We wear black. We exercise on the treadmill. We run into one another on the street or in the bookstores. I wind up talking a lot to big groups of women like us. One of my small securities is knowing that if I forget my reading glasses, there will probably be at least a dozen people in the audience who have the same magnification number I have bought at a drugstore like mine.

All the 2.0s—could you raise your hands? Thank you. See. Us.

One of the things we all have in common is that we've lived through the greatest social/political revolution in the last century in this country, and that is the rebirth of feminism, and the subsequent extraordinary change in the lives of women like us, and our daughters and granddaughters. When we were growing up, there were no girls in Little League. There were no altar girls. Most Wall Street law firms had never had a woman partner. Most hospitals had never had a female surgical resident. There were no women in the Senate or on the Supreme Court, and Great Britain had never had a woman prime minister. I could never have imagined how different the world would be by the time I was pushing fifty. I could never have imagined that we would come to take for granted women cops and firefighters, women rabbis and ministers, women senators and women judges, women partners and women surgeons, women editors and women columnists.

I could never have imagined that my boys, when little, would be talking in the backseat of the car one day driving home from a visit to my friend the pediatrician, and that Chris would say to Quin, "When I get big I might want to be a doctor." And Quin would reply, "Don't be stupid, Christopher, only girls can be doctors."

I could never have imagined that trickle-down feminism would become so pervasive that some of the things we thought of as utopian or idealistic twenty years ago today would become part of the culture, so that one day, when I was visiting a junior high school in Queens, one beleaguered boy would rise to his feet and begin a question, "Okay, I know that girls can do anything boys can, but . . ."

He thought it was nothing, what he was saying. He thought it was a truism, a universally accepted fact. Girls can do anything boys can.

I heard the greatest social revolution in the history of the twentieth century encapsulated in that offhand introduction.

Okay, I know girls can do anything boys can, but . . .

Well, here's the but, my friends, and perhaps the beginning of the millennium is a good time to deconstruct it.

Was the point of this great social revolution to have corner offices, executive washrooms, fat retainers, and retirement accounts?

Did we want the right to lead imitation men's lives? Or did we really want something that we haven't quite begun to get yet, the right to put our grand stamp on the ethos of the whole wide world?

The modern feminist movement over the last thirty years was a dialectic. We started out with a thesis, the thesis of wife and mother, what Betty Friedan, exactly forty years ago, named the "feminine mystique."

And we fashioned an antithesis, and not to be coy about it, it was too often a kind of faux man's life, complete with those little floppy tie things with our suits that almost did us all in.

Lately, we've approached a synthesis, a balance. And that is that work, influence, even power with no countervailing forces, no intimacy, no family, no sense of connection to others, is for many of us no kind of life at all.

We women know what matters, once we combine our demands for equality with our desire for meaning. That is why women have, throughout their lives, known precisely how to give back, whether it was to share with their children the books they'd read as children themselves, to share with their friends the mistakes they had made and the hard times they had seen, to share with their aging parents the love and care they had once known themselves. Whether we had means or not, we women have always been philanthropists, creating the entire world out of bit upon bit of what sometimes seems like a bottomless well of personal individual generosity.

The great social revolution of the last thirty years meant that we rebelled against the indiscriminate taking of those things we had to give. We rebelled against being taken for granted, as support and as caregiver. We rebelled against being seen as second-class citizens because we had done the discredited work of creating and launching a new generation of human beings.

And we finally found ourselves where we belonged, and that was everywhere.

But with great gains we must always be careful of our potential losses, and if we become the sort of people who believe, as a group, that the position of your name on the page or the letterhead is the most important thing about you, we will, as the Bible verse goes, have gained the whole world and lost our own souls.

If this great social revolution is about us, it's nowhere near enough. There are other women whose lives have not changed as ours have, who continue to live swaddled in burkas or enslaved by male tradition, who bear children they cannot feed and have no safeguard against bearing children they do not want. Here is their résumé, in sum: 80 percent of the world's 35 million refugees and displaced people are women and children.

You can't call yourself a feminist if you think of all those lost and wandering women and are not moved.

You cannot call yourself a mother if you think of all those lost and wandering children and are not moved.

You cannot call yourself a human being if you think of all those lost and wandering people and are not moved.

They do, in their fractured lives, what women have always done. They comfort and care. They give shape and sustenance. As Kofi Annan once said, "They maintain the social fabric."

Imagine doing that alone, amid the wreckage of war, in a strange place with old people and young depending upon you alone. It puts the glass ceiling in stark contrast to the dirt floor and the walls bombed, broken, gone for now, perhaps for good.

My mother, who just missed the revolution that changed our lives, left her five children an index card on which she had written in pencil this section of Saint Paul's letters to the Corinthians:

Though I speak with the tongues of men and of angels and have not love, I am sounding brass or a clanging cymbal. Though I have the gift of prophecy and know all things, though I have faith strong enough to move mountains, but am without love, I am nothing.

Love is patient, love is kind, love is not jealous. Love is never boastful, conceited or rude; never selfish, not quick to take offense. Love is not vengeful; does not gloat over the sins of others but delights in the truth.

Love bears all things, believes all things, hopes all things, endures all things.

Love never fails.

In some versions of the New Testament, the word "love" is translated as charity, which suits our purposes today. What does it profit us if we gain all that résumé power but have not love within or charity toward our fellows without? Doesn't that mean, essentially, that the price of equality will have been the loss, if not of femininity, than of humanity?

Most of us in this room have done well in our lives. It is fine to want to do well. But if we do not do good, too, doing well is simply not enough.

We changed the world over the last three decades. My daughter assumes access and opportunities that would never have occurred to me. She has grown up in a world in which it is possible to watch the secretary of state give a news conference and to critique her choice of scarf and brooch. She has grown up in a world in which she watched both figure skating and the women's ice hockey team when she watched the Olympics. She has grown up in a world in which, at a black-tie dinner one night, I heard her say sweetly to the woman on her left, oh, you're my second female astronaut.

And she has grown up in a world in which millions of women in one part of the world have extraordinary opportunity, and millions of others have no place for themselves and their children to live. Think of what our homes mean to all of us. Think about losing home, leaving it, perhaps never to see it again. Think about feeling both overwhelmed by the task of maintaining a family under those conditions, and impotent because all of the power of resolution and decision-making was in the hands of others.

Many of you are women with power—the power of influence and the power of affluence. Perhaps you should walk out of this room today with a shadow at your heels, the shadow of a woman who is really one of us, a woman in Afghanistan, in Bosnia, in Angola. Perhaps she will remind each of us of what we've been given and what we have to give in return. The point was not the corner office. The point was sisterhood, solidarity, freedom, and peace. The point was the whole wide world.

Off with Their Ties

I AM A FEMINIST, have been since I was seventeen years old, smart, ambitious, and really pissed off at what I took for an assumption of Y-chromosome privilege. I would like to be able to tell you that I became a feminist to make the world a better place for women, but the fact of the matter is that I wanted to make the world a better place for me.

Remember that this was in 1970, when grown women were still called "girls" as a matter of course. Remember that this was in the nascent days of the second stage of the women's movement in this country, a movement that had been becalmed, since suffrage, by two world wars and the resulting aftermath of embracing a sometimes stifling status quo. For a young woman galvanized by Betty Friedan's tales of smart women gone soft, it was easy to slip into the easiest sort of polarity, the either/or of victim and enemy, oppressed and oppressor.

Guys didn't get it. They were condescending, arrogant, overbearing, overweening. They were aggressive, violent, mean-spirited, psychologically stunted. There was enough truth in this, after centuries of women feeling held down and devalued, to set a tone in both our professional and personal lives.

For me all that ended on a very hot day in September. It happened to be September 11, but a September 11 without the terrible connotations, a September 11 almost nineteen years ago. I pushed and yelled. My husband wept. The lights on the ceiling were like silver suns. "It's a boy," someone said.

And thus we come to the second stage of the second stage of feminism. We come to it in different ways. We come to it when we realize that a gender revolution that includes only half the populace is no revolution at all. We come to it when we realize that most of our lives, in the workplace and at home, are going to be inextricably intertwined with the lives of men, whether they are our bosses, our employees, our brothers, our husbands, or simply our very good friends.

While we changed laws and institutions in the last thirty years, we sometimes did not change hearts and minds. And so, both as a feminist and the mother of two sons, it has come to me slowly but surely that the part of the promise of the women's movement that I hope to see fulfilled in the twenty-first century is the liberation of men.

For me this knowledge began with two beloved boys, born less than a year apart. Because when I looked at them I knew that they were facing a future of gender roles as constrained, in their own different way, as those in which we women had found ourselves tied up for so long. I was terrified of seeing their Technicolor characters crammed into some stiff-upper-lip, button-down-collar brown cardboard box of stereotypical masculinity. The parameters of what passed for maleness seemed so limiting.

They'll want trucks, one mother told me.

They'll run you ragged, said another.

They'll hit. They'll bite. They'll run. They'll run off and leave you later when they find some satisfactory girl substitute.

No one ever said, they'll be who they are. But that is who they became.

Femininity was once easy to define. It was: not masculine.

But all that changed when women moved out into new roles in the world, because some of the behaviors they needed and had always secretly had were ones that we had defined as masculine. Leadership, ambition, physical strength, mental toughness. The easy definition fell away, as well it should.

That left men with an old easy definition of masculinity: not feminine. But what could that possibly mean in a world that included Margaret Thatcher and Madonna, Venus and Serena Williams, Carly Fiorina and Oprah Winfrey? What could that mean in a world in which there was some likelihood that their wives would earn more than they did, a likelihood that some found curiously reassuring?

And had that "not feminine" definition cheated men out of too much over the years? Had men been required to follow a ladder while women were learning to follow their inclinations? If I believe, as I do, that the hands-on rearing of children was an enormous blessing to me, as both a human being and a writer, can I bear the thought that my sons may miss out on that because of some narrow and outmoded societal mandate associated with their gender?

I once wrote that a girl is like a Swiss watch, a boy like a sundial—more primitive, easier to read. But I know now that even that is an oversimplification, now that I've put in almost two decades on boy watch. I'm taken always by the oversimplifications and the contradictions. Why is it that boys seem to have such fast friendships when they are younger yet such cursory, emotionally distanced ones when they grow up? Why is the aggressive behavior of boys frowned upon when they are young and rewarded in the workplace?

In 1959, long before any resurgence of feminism, Selma Fraiberg described this in her classic explanation of the development of small children called *The Magic Years.*

"The standard for good behavior in the classroom is very often the girl standard," she wrote, and as a girl who never conformed to the girl standard and still hates to fold her hands, I can say with certainty that she was right. Yet the standard of behavior in the world is the boy standard: active, assertive, on the move. So the placid boy, the dreamy boy, the nurturing boy, the poetic boy, is often, even now, made to feel like a creature from outer space by an outside culture that still likes simpler standards of masculinity, while the wild boy, the outspoken boy, the profane boy, the hyperactive boy—all are marginalized by a school system that prizes order above all.

In other words, while girls have learned that they can be anything, boys are learning that nothing they do is really right. And that's really wrong.

The answer is simple in theory and enormously difficult in practice. It happens to be the philosophy that was truly the linchpin of feminism, once all the sloganeering was cleared away. It was the deep and enduring belief that people be permitted to define themselves, not just by gender but by ability, inclination, and character.

This is difficult, but it is doable. Because while surmounting other stereotypes, racial or ethnic ones, requires us to give the benefit of the doubt to those we do not really know with issues we cannot really personally apprehend, gender is different. Nearly all of us not only know, but live with or have lived with a member of the opposite sex. In most cases, if not all, we have not only lived with them, we have loved them. And because of that we are inclined, by love, to enlarge opportunity, not to foreshorten it.

Unless, of course, love is hamstrung by fear. We want our children to become their best selves, but we are terrified that if they are too far outside the norm it will cause them discomfort, even pain. And we are afraid that if they are too different than we are, they will disdain and even forget us.

What it means to be male has changed and will change because what it means to be female has changed forever, and the two are interlocking parts. We want our boys to be who they are, not to suffer the pain and indignity of masquerade their whole lives long. I realized that on the steamy September day a doctor handed me the future, and I realized that what I really had been working toward was the impulse to make the world a better place for everyone, male and female alike. The feminist movement broke the hard cold ice of gender stereotypes for us all. It can be hard to swim when you are used to skating. But the alternative is drowning.

Oh, Godot

ONE NIGHT I BROUGHT MY DAUGHTER and her friend Claire to a production of *Waiting for Godot* in which my eldest son was appearing. And when the lights came up after that shattering last scene, when Vladimir and Estragon are still exactly where they started, the look on eleven-year-old Claire's face was comical.

"Godot never came," she said, with wonder and a hint of existential despair that I'm sure would have thrilled Samuel Beckett, if indeed he was ever thrilled about anything.

Apparently Claire was one of the last people in the world to understand the trick of *Godot*—that is, that two hapless fools, or seekers, or lost souls, or whatever you consider them, wait throughout the entire play for someone, something, that never arrives. Perhaps it is their salvation. Perhaps, as the name suggests, it's the Deity. Perhaps it's just a source of direction and guidance and self-knowledge. Whatever it is, it is everything, and when the curtain comes down, it is still missing in action.

Well, I am here today with a piece of good news in honor of this graduation day. Godot has arrived. The linchpin, the bedrock, the source of all the questions that have plagued your soul, and all the answers, too. The way is clear. The way is here. You saw Godot when you blew your hair dry this morning, when you brushed your teeth and put on mascara.

I have seen your salvation, and it is you, staring back at yourself, your eyes windows to your heart and mind.

Many of you have looked for Godot, or some facsimile, elsewhere in this particular place. You have looked for it in the grade on the last page of that art history paper, in the grad school acceptance letters, in the laughter of your friends, in the smile of some nice man or woman. What passed for your life was often a search for outside validation. Law school or a museum internship would save you, or love or romance or sex, or a poem published in a magazine, a painting hung at a show.

But one edition of a magazine has a way of giving way to another, and course grades come and go, and occasionally, very occasionally, a lover who should know better will nonetheless dump you. The prizes arrive, but soon they are dusty, and then what do you have?

You better have you. The real you, the authentic examined self, not some patchwork collection of affectations and expectations, mores and mannerisms, some treadmill set to the prevailing speed of universal acceptability, the tyranny of homogeny, whether the homogeny of the straight world of the suits or the spiky world of the avant-garde.

The tyrant must be overthrown, the lockstep unlocked. Today is the day that those lucky enough to be your teachers, your classmates, your friends, and your parents must say: Your life belongs in full to you and you alone. Do not cede it to anyone else, no matter how loving or well intentioned.

People will tell you what you ought to study and how you ought to feel. They will tell you what to read and how to live. They will urge you to take jobs they themselves loathe and to follow safe paths they themselves find tedious.

Don't listen.

This is tough stuff. It's so much easier to follow the template, to walk the straight and narrow set out by the culture, the family, the friends, the focus groups. You will have to bend all your will not to march to the music that all of those great "theys" there pipe on their flutes. They want you to go to professional school, to pierce your navel, to wear khakis, to tint your hair, to bare your soul. These are the fashionable ways. The music is tinny, if you listen close enough. Look inside, look inside.

This will always be your struggle. I know this from experience. When I quit *The New York Times* to be a full-time mother, the voices of the world said that I was nuts. When I quit it again to be a full-time novelist, they said I was nuts again. But I am not nuts. I am successful on my own terms. Because if your success is not on your own terms, if it looks good to the world but does not feel good in your soul, it is not success at all.

Look at your fingers. Each one is crowned by an abstract design that is completely different from that of anyone in this crowd, in this country, in this world. They are a metaphor for everything. Each of you is as different as your fingerprints. Why should you march to any lockstep? Our love of lockstep is our greatest curse, the source of all that bedevils us. It is the source of homophobia, xenophobia, racism, sexism, terrorism, bigotry of every variety and hue, because it tells us there is one right way to do things, to look, to behave, to feel, when the only right way is to feel your heart hammering inside you and to listen to what its timpani is saying.

James Joyce lived most of his writing life in grinding poverty, cadging off friends. One critic called *The Catcher in the Rye* "a small book" and referred to Holden Caulfield as a delinquent. Why did Wallace Stevens work all day as an insurance company executive and then, on weekends, sit down and write poems like the one that ends "Only here and there, an old sailor, drunk and asleep in his boots, catches tigers in red weather," knowing, surely knowing, that at the country club in Connecticut his compatriots would gather after golf to say "What the hell?"

He must have looked in the mirror, and looking back, seen a poet, surely. Seen himself, as Salinger did, as Joyce did. As you must, as we all must, if we are to be more than dead men walking.

You already know this. I just need to remind you. Think back. Think back to first grade, when you could still hear the sound of your own voice in your head, when you were too young, too unformed, too fantastic to understand that you were supposed to take on the protective coloration of the expectations of those around you. Think of what the writer Catherine Drinker Bowen once wrote, more than half a century ago: "Many a man who has known himself at ten forgets himself utterly between ten and thirty."

Many a woman, too.

You are not alone in this. We parents have forgotten our way sometimes, too. When you were first born, each of you, our great glory was in thinking you absolutely distinct from every baby who had ever been born before. You were a miracle of singularity, and we knew it in every fiber of our being. You shouted "Dog." You lurched across the playground. You put a scrawl of red paint next to a squiggle of green and we put it on the fridge and said, Ohmigod, ohmigod, you are a painter a poet a prodigy a genius.

But we are only human, and being a parent is a very difficult job, more difficult than any other, because it is twenty-four/seven, because it is unpaid and unrewarded much of the time, because it requires the shaping of other people, which is an act of extraordinary hubris. And over the years we learned to want for you things that you did not necessarily want for yourself. We learned to want the lead in the play, the acceptance to our own college, the straight and narrow path that sometimes leads absolutely nowhere. We learned to suspect, even fear your differences, not to celebrate them. Sometimes we were convinced conformity would make life better, or at least easier for you. Sometimes we had a hard time figuring out where you ended and we began.

Guide us back to where we started. Help us not to make mistakes out of fear or out of love. Teach us as gently as we once taught you about who you really are and who you intend to become. Learn not to listen to us when we are wrong. Whether you are twenty-four or fifty-four, begin today to say no to the Greek chorus that thinks it knows the parameters of a happy life when all it knows is the homogenization of human experience.

Vladimir and Estragon—they just wait and wait for some formless enormous something. And sadly enough, that's what some of us wind up doing in our own lives: waiting for the promotion, or the mate, or the bonus, or the honor, or the children, that will somehow make us real to our own selves. "You did see me, didn't you?" Vladimir asks Godot's messenger, as though he does not exist unless he registers in other eyes, as though his soul is made of smoke instead of steel.

That is his despair. That is his torment. Learn from him. You are only real if you can see yourself, see yourself clear and true in the mirror of your soul and smile upon the reflection. Samuel Butler once said, "Life is like playing a violin solo in public, and learning the instrument as one goes on." That sounds terrifying, doesn't it, and difficult, too. But that way lies music. Look in the mirror. Who is that man? Who is that woman? She is the work of your life; he is its greatest glory, too. Do not dare to dis them by dressing them up in someone else's spiritual clothing. Pick up your violin. Lift your bow. And play. Play your heart out.

5 Soul

THE FIRST THING I ALWAYS tell the students is how much I hate to write. The classrooms, no matter where they are, up a broken stretch of pavement in Brooklyn, ringed by pretty playing fields in Connecticut, are instantly familiar to me, the smell of chalk dust, industrial cleanser, Elmer's glue, steamed food, wet socks, the sense of somnolent boredom, unprepared terror, and a hint of excitement waiting to be woken, like a cat sleeping beneath each desk.

It is the familiarity that makes me feel so close to each of them, so anxious that they understand that what I do, which is the bedrock of what they must learn, is not easy. A writer never came to visit when I was in school; I thought of writers as elderly men with beards, British mainly, with sonorous voices, not too terribly different from the way I thought of God. (I thought of George Eliot this way, too. I think I had read *Middlemarch* twice before I discovered that George Eliot was a woman.) I knew, by reading their wonderfully wrought prose, that writing must be easy for them. Fountain pens, rolltop desks, certainty.

That's why I always tell the students how much I hate to write. Even the students who are accomplished, who get the A's, who submit to the school paper or the literary magazine, suspect that if they were really good at it, good enough to make a living, it would be easier. It's important to let them know that it is never easy, even for those who are obliged to do it with some regularity. I say "obliged" because the truth is that a combination of laziness and fear would probably lead me to constant inaction had I not promised a succession of editors that I would fill their empty pages.

"So why do you do it?" one smart kid asked at a school in New Jersey one morning.

"To pay the mortgage," I said flippantly.

I backtracked on that answer almost as soon as it was out of my mouth because I did not want to mislead those eighth graders, with their notebooks rich with graffiti and their watchful eyes. I didn't want to mislead them any more than I wanted them to be misled into thinking that sitting down and producing a poem or a paper or a novel or a column was ever without fear and loathing. Finally I said, "Think of it as a letter to yourself."

Because that's what it is, the work I produce, the succession of columns that mark the year as surely as the school calendar, the Christmas column on consumerism, the July column on summer reading, the columns that mark various Tuesdays on which elections are held. Of course they are designed to speak to readers, to share a perspective on issues and events, to offer information and experience, and, sometimes, to try to compel and cajole into consensus. But inevitably those columns change and shape me, too, so that at the end of a given year I feel as if my mind has been subtly sculpted by each one.

That's why it is oversimplification when I talk about hating to write. What I mean is that the blank page is always a rebuke and a challenge. It is like being one of those people in the movies with amnesia, lying in a hospital bed in a flat featureless landscape of white: Who am I? Where do I belong? The purpose of the exercise comes when the white gives way to the words, when one after another a sentence appears under my frantic fingers, those fingers that long ago lost a conscious sense of where the letters lie and now only have some weird synaptical relation between a thought and a keystroke.

The funny thing is that it has rarely been the big columns, on the big issues, that answer the questions of identity and purpose that I am covertly posing to myself. At the end of a well-reasoned piece on abortion or the ordination of women, I sometimes wind up thinking about that particular issue in a way I have not done before, and my hope is that the same will be true of the reader. But the back roads of experience take me where I need to go as a human being. Sometimes they are quirky and amusing and remind me of how silly we all can be, in our fads and our enthusiasms. Sometimes they are as important as life and death.

Those students ask me if I keep a journal. I am always a little abashed to admit that I never have. At a fairly young age, I began to trade words for money. (Putting it that way makes it sound like the most high-minded of prostitutions. Which I suppose in some fashion it is.) And ever since I have insisted on getting paid if I am going to force myself to fill a blank page, given how much terror it inspires.

But still I urge them to write, uncompensated, even if they have no plans to become writers, for one reason only, and that is to know themselves, for now and for later. Their written words are their personal histories, as they have been mine. They bring the past vividly alive within the square diorama of the page. And that has been a great blessing, the gift I give myself, that keeps on giving.

Life After Death

MAY 1994

MY GREAT JOURNALISTIC CONTRIBUTION to my family is that I write obituaries. First my mother's, twenty-two years ago, listing her accomplishments: two daughters, three sons. Then that of my father's second wife, dead of the same disease that killed his first one.

Last week it was my sister-in-law. "Sherry Quindlen, 41," I tapped out on the keyboard, and then it was real, like a last breath. "When you write about me," she said one day in the hospital, "be nice."

For the obit I could only be accurate. The limitations of the form eliminate the more subjective truths: a good heart, a generous soul, who made her living taking care of other people's children. My brother's wife, the mother of a teenager and a toddler, who went from a bad cough to what was mistakenly said to be pneumonia to what was correctly diagnosed as lung and liver cancer, from fall to spring, from the day she threw a surprise fortieth birthday party for her husband to the day he chose her casket.

Only days after the funeral her two daughters were shopping together when a saleswoman looked at them and said admiringly, "Your mother must have beautiful hair."

"Yes she does," said the elder, who had learned quickly what is expected of survivors.

Grief remains one of the few things that has the power to silence us. It is a whisper in the world and a clamor within. More than sex, more than faith, even more than its usher death, grief is unspoken, publicly ignored except for those moments at the funeral that are over too quickly, or the conversations among the cognoscenti, those of us who recognize in one another a kindred chasm deep in the center of who we are.

Maybe we do not speak of it because death will mark all of us, sooner or later. Or maybe it is unspoken because grief is only the first part of it. After a time it becomes something less sharp but larger, too, a more enduring thing called loss.

Perhaps that is why this is the least explored passage: because it has no end. The world loves closure, loves a thing that can, as they say, be gotten through. This is why it comes as a great surprise to find that loss is forever, that two decades after the event there are those occasions when something in you cries out at the continuous presence of an absence. "An awful leisure," Emily Dickinson once called what the living have after death.

Sherwin Nuland, a doctor and professor at Yale, has become an unlikely bestselling author with a straightforward, unsparing yet deeply human description of the end of life entitled *How We Die.* In the introduction he explains that he has written the book "to demythologize the process of dying."

But I wondered, reading on, if he was doing something else as well. He wrote: "My mother died of colon cancer one week after my eleventh birthday, and that fact has shaped my life. All that I have become and much that I have not become, I trace directly or indirectly to her death."

Loss as muse. Loss as character. Loss as life. When the president talks of moving some days to the phone to call his mother, who died in January, he is breaking a silence about what so many have felt. "The hard part is for those of us who've kept silent for decades to start talking about our losses," Hope Edelman writes in her new book, *Motherless Daughters*. Yet how second nature the silence becomes, so much a rule of etiquette that a fifteen-year-old knows when her loss is as raw as a freshly dug grave not to discomfit a stranger by revealing it in passing.

All that she and her sister will become, and much they will not, will be traced later on to a time when spring had finally passed over the threshold of winter and the cemetery drives were edged with pink tulips, shivering slightly in a chill April rain. My brother and I know too much about their future; both teenagers when our mother died, we know that if the girls were to ask us, "When does it stop hurting?" we would have to answer, in all candor, "If it ever does, we will let you know."

The landscapes of all our lives become as full of craters as the surface of the moon. My brother is a young widower with young children, as his father was before him. And I write my obituaries carefully and think about how little the facts suffice, not only to describe the dead but to tell what they will mean to the living all the rest of our lives. We are defined by whom we have lost. "Don't let them forget me," Sherry said. Oh, hon, piece of cake.

Anniversary

JANUARY 1997

I NEEDED MY MOTHER AGAIN the other day. This time it was a fairly serious matter, a question from my doctor about our family medical history. Most of the time what I want is more trivial: the name of the family that lived next to us on Kenwood Road, the fate of that black wool party dress with the killer neckline, curiosity about whether those tears were real or calculated to keep all five of us in line. "When Mom cried, man," my brother Bob said not long ago. "That's what I really couldn't handle."

I've needed my mother many many times over the last twenty-five years, but she has never been there, except in my mind, where she tells me to buy quality, keep my hair off my face, and give my father the benefit of the doubt. When Bob's wife was dying of cancer several years ago, we made her make video- and audiotapes for her children because our little sister, who was eight when our own mother died, cannot remember what Prudence Marguerite Pantano Quindlen looked or sounded like. I remember. I remember everything. I was nineteen; I was older. I am older now by five years than my mother was when she died. Her death transformed my life.

We're different, those of us whose mothers have gone and left us to fend for ourselves. For that is what we wind up doing, no matter how good our fathers, or family, or friends: On some deep emotional level, we fend for ourselves. The simplest way to say it is also the most true—we are the world's grown-ups. "No girl becomes a woman until her mother dies" goes an old proverb. No matter what others may see, or she herself thinks, we believe down to our bones that our mother's greatest calling was us; with that fulcrum to our lives gone, we become adults overnight.

This makes some of us hard, sometimes, and driven, too. We perform for a theater of empty seats: Look at me, Ma, I did good, I'm okay, I'll get by. It was no surprise to me to discover that Madonna's mother died when she was a child. Rosie O'Donnell used to watch the old talk shows, Mike Douglas, Merv Griffin, with her mom before her mom died when she was a kid. I don't know Rosie O'Donnell, but I know whom she thinks of every time she steps through those curtains and onto that stage and hears the applause. Maybe she hears the sound of two hands clapping, the two that are not there, the only ones that count.

The funny thing is that the loss makes us good and happy people in some ways, too, in love with life because we know how fleeting and how precious it can be. We have our priorities straight. When I quit a great job as a columnist because I wanted to take up another great job as a novelist, lots of readers couldn't understand why I would give up a public forum for a quieter, more private one. The answer was simple: I wanted to. But I knew to do what I wanted, when I wanted, because I know that today is the only certainty I possess. I'm pretty sure I'll be a woman who'll die without regrets. My mother left me that, along with her engagement ring. Someone stole it when they burglarized my apartment when I was twenty-five. At the time I was enraged, bereft, inconsolable. Of course, none of that had to do with the ring.

There's just a hole in my heart, and nothing to plug it. The truth is that there's no one, ever, in your life like your mother. And that's even if she's a bad mother, punitive, critical. Your mother is the mirror. Whether you elect to gaze at the reflection with equanimity, to tilt the glass or crack it outright, it is the point from which you always begin. It is who you are. When the English princes, those poor boys, lost their mother at the end of summer, walking through the quiet streets of London behind her coffin when they should have been leaving for school, the commentators talked about how she had brought emotion and warmth into their lives in a way their father had not, could not. But that was not just the nature of Diana; it is the nature of many of our families. What a father brings, in most cases, is something different, more like a relationship, less like an atmosphere. He is a human being, she the bedrock of existence, the foundation of our house. That may be an oversimplification, but I think there is a lot of truth in it. Certainly it is true to say that my father was nearly as lost without his wife as we were without our mother. The difference was that for the widower there is an antidote called marriage. The motherless are motherless for life.

Sometimes, missing my mother, I lose track of whether I am missing a human being or a way of life. Our mothers only slowly become people to us, as we grow older and they do, too. But for years and years they are both more and less than that. First they are warmth and food and an inchoate sense of security, then cheerleader and overseer, then finally listener, perhaps even friend. Our family was a wheel; she was the hub. Without her we fell apart, a collection of sticks. We've knit back together, some of us, as adults, but it has never really been the same.

There is something primitive about this love and this loss. What does it mean, to sleep beneath the heart of another person, safe and warm, for almost a year? No scientist can truly say. But it must have some visceral power that we cannot really understand, only intuit. She was the only person who ever loved me unconditionally. That was her great gift, too. It has been the bulwark of my life, has made everything else possible. When I can see myself refracted through the rosy lens of my mother's love, it melts the self-doubt and brings to life the tiny sanctuary lamp of confidence.

Since my mother, by almost any objective measure I possess today, was a good mother, I try every day to wake up and be like her for the sake of my children. This is her third, perhaps her most important gift to me. And the gift our children give us, of course, is the feeling that we are no longer a dead end, that while our line is truncated in one direction it now extends in another. That is why some of the ice inside us melts and breaks when we who have lost our mothers become mothers ourselves. My daughter looks so much like my mother; that is a great joy to me.

"Oh, Mommy, I feel so sorry for you, that your mommy is dead," she said to me one night, leaning into me, her head against my heart. For a moment I thought to say, it was a long time ago, or I don't mind so much anymore, or I get along just fine, one of those things we say when we pretend that what we feel doesn't matter. Finally I just said, "Thank you."

My children may not really understand what it feels like, what happened to me. And I hope they never will. Oh, I know someday they will lose their mother, as I did mine, but I hope it is when they are safely cushioned by years of love and life together, by spouses and children and the knowledge that they have learned everything I have to teach. None of us had that, when our mother died. We were too young to really know her and too young to learn to live without her. One of the hardest things for my brother, when his wife was dying, was knowing firsthand what her loss would mean to her daughters, one a toddler, the other a teenager. Neither knew the depth of the chasm in the landscape of their lives. But Bob knew, from experience.

I suspect my children know instinctively that losing me would be, in some fashion, like losing their own lives. It would be like coming home to find a hole in the ground where the house once stood, to look into the hole and ask, where in the world do I go now? When I watched the Princess of Wales's sons walking with their heads down along her funeral route, I wanted to reach through the screen and touch their shoulders, to say, "It will be all right." But I know that is a lie. I know even when things are finally all right for them, they will never really be all right again.

It's been twenty-five years, and I can even joke about it now, in a macabre way. I refuse to go and see what I call "dead mother movies"; I can watch *Terms of Endearment* when it comes on television until Debra Winger goes to the hospital, and then I'm out of there. I only go to my mother's grave when I attend family funerals. I don't see the point; she's not in there. She's in me, the way I was once in her, only not as tangible. Inspirational books would have us believe that that is sufficient. That is such utter nonsense that my lip curls just writing the words. Because here is the final thing about having your mother die: You never, ever get used to it. You want her back. Or at least I do.

It never would have occurred to me, sitting in her living room twenty-five years ago, trying to decide what to do with her clothes, that all these years later I would learn what I've learned from her death, about being a good person and a good mother. It never would have occurred to me that it would make me so strong that I would go far and fast and not crash beneath the weight of some of the pressures that came with that. And it would never in a million years have occurred to me that twenty-five years later I would be sitting here writing about all this, the dishwasher and the dryer running, my three wonderful children at school, with tears running down onto my sweater as I realize that I would trade all I've learned for what I lost so long ago.

Leg Waxing and
Life Everlasting

APRIL 2001

MY MOTHER DID NOT EXFOLIATE. In her medicine cabinet she had a big white jar of Pond's cold cream and a big blue jar of Noxzema. That's as much care and feeding as her face ever got. As for my grandmothers, the one with skin like tissue paper and the one with skin like saddle leather: I imagine soap and water did the job.

How surprised those women would be to discover the amount of maintenance the human face requires today. Exfoliation, antioxidizing, moisturizing, revitalizing, and toning. Retinol, alpha hydroxy, plant estrogens, and herbal peels. This is why the cosmetic business had sales of almost $7 billion last year, because a sizable number of us, in tending our bodies, have lost our minds.

Simple self-reliance has given way to a team approach: stylists, colorists, trainers, facialists, waxers. ("The most famous waxer in New York," says Leah, one of the army of Russian immigrant women who ply the beauty trade in Manhattan, as though she were Rembrandt and a hairy calf her canvas.) In two decades I went from a person who got by with a bar of Ivory and a bottle of Pert Plus to someone who has accumulated mousse, gel, pomade, volumizers, buffers, bronzers, and polishers. The shower looks like a salad bar: banana and papaya conditioners, mint and basil shampoos. In the New York metropolitan area alone, there are four thousand Korean nail parlors, which offer silk wraps, acrylic wraps, nail tips, manicures, and pedicures. My friend Joan says that her mother has never had a pedicure because she does not want another human being sitting at her feet. This is obviously not a widespread sentiment.

It's popular to insist that all this is the purview of a spoiled bourgeoisie, Joan Rivers by way of Ivana Trump. But there is as much navel-gazing on QVC as in Neiman Marcus or at Canyon Ranch. Nighttime soaps actress Victoria Principal says brightly in a cable infomercial promoting her eponymous line of skin care products, "It's science's answer to the Fountain of Youth." Worth noting: Ponce de León himself found only Florida.

Every cheesy commercial is for a miracle enzyme that eats fat or a paste that removes troublesome facial hair; every cable network has a woman leading others like her in the dance of cardio fitness meant to mimic actual activity. (Or, as the farmer in Pennsylvania once said when he saw me power walking, "You wouldn't have to bother with that if you'd do a day's work.") There is not only exercise; there is a professional class of people to assist in exercise, to correct the form, to count the reps, to adjust the weight. Cross-training shoes, yoga pants, pulse monitors. Pecs, delts, glutes. The world is full of amateur anatomists studying their own musculature, and products that didn't even exist ten years ago.

Perhaps this is a function of hyperannuated vanity, the feeling that the face is infinitely more desirable and important than anything lurking in the mind behind it. Perhaps Americans have become self-obsessive, unable to see past their own gleaming white incisors and painted toes. Hair plugs, Botox, collagen, dermabrasion: Perhaps what all this really reflects is a fear of death. (Think about that the next time you're having your hair highlighted.) Taken together, the rise of the funeral parlor, the invention of the StairMaster, and the ascendancy of the low-fat diet have had this pernicious effect: the subconscious belief that we will live forever.

Mortality was once a more integral part of everyday life than hair care products, and a more natural one, too. Young people and old ones, the suddenly ill and the chronically infirm, died in their beds at home and were laid out in the parlor, carried to the church, and buried in the churchyard by the people who loved them. In most towns and neighborhoods, there was one very old woman who lived into her nineties, outlived her children and their children, too. Death was a part of life.

But many childhood diseases have been cured, thank God, and life expectancy stretches into the seventies, and a significant number of Americans are now over the age of ninety. And mortality no longer dwells among us. People who become ill are whisked away to hospitals to die out of sight, and people who die are whisked away to funeral homes, to be reincarnated briefly as waxen overdressed versions of themselves. Death seems, not part of life, but a brief interruption stage-managed by strangers in suits, so that it scarcely seems real at all. As Jessica Mitford described it in her classic accusation of a book, *The American Way of Death*, the end of life has become a "grotesque cloud-cuckooland where the trappings of Gracious Living are transformed, as in a nightmare, into the trappings of Gracious Dying." It would be little wonder if there was a creeping belief that such an anemic process, all appearance, no reality, could be forestalled indefinitely by light weights and high fiber.

The youth produced by scalpel and laser is of a particularly arid sort, as much like the bloom of the real thing as the décor of those funeral homes is like a real live living room. But if the abs are tight, the eyes unlined, the hands unspotted, the hairline intact, if fifty-five is the new forty, then can't the inevitable be, if not avoided, at least indefinitely deferred? The answer is, of course, no. As Jacqueline Kennedy Onassis was said to have told a friend when she became ill, "Why in the world did I do all those push-ups?"

Nonetheless the greatest growth industry in this country is the one dedicated to the mirage of good grooming as the road to immortality. Immigrants past built bridges and schools, gilded the cherubim in the corner of churches. Today an entire immigrant class makes a living painting toenails and opening pores. Advances in science and medicine have combined to offer this: the tattooing of permanent eye liner, the bleaching of teeth, the lasering of sun spots. The waning days of a great nation can only be charted in hindsight. But surely it is a danger sign of some sort when a country is no longer able to care for its own cuticles.

Watching the
World Go By

FEBRUARY 2001

NEVER WATCHED *SURVIVOR*. Never will. What's the point? I've eaten bugs inadvertently myself, dozing in the hammock by the pond on a muggy summer evening. And anyone who wants to watch two pitched and petty rival factions go at one another can just wander between the purchasing and accounting departments of any company. Add up the physical challenges and the head games, and the whole thing sounds like nothing more than gym class meets sophomore mixer, no scarier than high school. (Although in the last analysis, nothing is scarier than high school.) I don't scare easy. I've lived through a kitchen renovation in an old house with uneven floorboards, and Donald Trump is building a skyscraper at the end of my block. Here on Temptation Island, where multimillionaire divorce lawyers roam free, survivors are those who pass the co-op board.

People named Kimmi and Colby and Amber (who chooses the participants, the writers for *One Life to Live*?) balancing on rafts, living on goat brains, turning brown in the outback? This is a stunt, not survival. Liz Taylor and Debbie Reynolds doing a TV movie and making fun of Eddie Fisher, Debbie still with that tight-lipped good-girl look—that's surviving. Bill Clinton taking an overdose of stupid pills, making an endless string of what we moms call "bad choices," then being lionized on the streets of Harlem after he decides to seek salvation and office space in an all-black neighborhood—that's surviving.

Yet how quickly the voyeurism of sofa slugs has become, not only a national obsession but an expected staple of the weekly program schedule. Only three decades ago America was shocked and amazed by the Loud family of Santa Barbara, California, who permitted a documentary crew to plaster their imperfect lives on public television in a series called *An American Family.* Today the fractured marriages of ordinary folk are severed in the seedy real-life setting of *Divorce Court,* and the people who bring you *Trauma: Life in the ER* find themselves blurring the genital area of a patient while the camera comes in tight on his severed leg.

A very wise trial attorney, knowing of my unslakable appetite for episodes of *Law & Order* (particularly during the classic Chris Noth years) once remarked that a televised trial is as much like the real thing as a wedding is like a marriage. All the boring bits are excised, leaving only the high drama. And that's the same relationship between reality and reality TV. The broadcast version covers only the peaks and valleys, the breakups and the big events. The magic moment of birth without the tedium of toilet training. The white dress and the cutaway, not the socks on the bedroom floor. MTV's *The Real World* features more pitched arguments and aberrant hookups in a few weeks than most of us experience in a lifetime.

Conventional wisdom is that TV is the purview of those with nothing better to do. But this boom in the vicarious is instead the hallmark of a people with not enough time on their hands, people who have a to-do list instead of a life, people for whom the download can never be quick enough. An entire nation living at warp speed has no time for tedium. What could be easier than cutting out the middleman of our own daily existence and instead watching the high points of life on tape? All the passion, none of the pain or perspiration. When Bob Vila builds a deck, it gets built in only an episode, and the wood never warps.

Perhaps *Survivor* satisfies a stunted yen for adventure, or maybe its tribes are just stand-ins for the Machiavellian maneuvering of virtually every workplace, the intrigue without the bad coffee. It doesn't seem like particularly real reality television, although it's become the standard-bearer of the form. *A Baby Story*, on TLC, in which you get to see the precise moment when a woman says to her husband, "I hate you, I want the epidural" is reality TV. Or *Cops*, in which law-abiding Americans learn that suspects will never, ever quietly put their hands behind their backs for the cuffs (and that most police officers are way out of shape). Or even *The Operation*, which is a completely no-frills look at the miracles of medicine. Guess what? Mitral valve replacement surgery is as boring as watching paint dry.

Which leads us to the most terrifying reality show on television, more terrifying than watching Judge Judy yell at a grandmother who let her dog off the leash, more terrifying than seeing two girls with bad bleach jobs fight over the sexual favors of a round-shouldered guy with acne and a mullet cut on Ricki Lake, more terrifying than the salad-to-dessert C-SPAN broadcast of Katherine Harris giving a lunch speech in front of a portrait of Pat Nixon. *Trading Spaces* lets you watch as neighbors swap homes and, with the help of two annoying decorators who describe window treatments as fun, and a hunky carpenter who's always around (all right, it's only partly real), redo a room in the house next door. The episode in which the cheerful married couple painted the bedroom of the single father black to give it a manly, sophisticated look is not for the easily frightened.

Once there were visions of television uniting people, making the rich understand the problems of the poor, the poor understand the problems of the rich. (See: *Dynasty.*) A global community would develop around the cathode-ray tube. Instead it has come to this: bad bridesmaids' dresses, small-claims court, and stitches in some kid's lip up close and personal. And a black bedroom with this poor guy standing in the doorway making that face people make when they've gotten novelty sweatshirts for Christmas, the face that says "it's awful" so much better than words alone can say. Reality television is the twenty-first-century equivalent of astronaut food: Just point and click, and it's as though you're really alive. "I hate television. I hate it as much as peanuts. But I can't stop eating peanuts," Orson Welles once said. Pass the snacks and settle back. And if your kids want to talk or your mother calls just say, "Shhhh—they're about to vote someone off the island." Because isn't that what life is really all about?

Aha!
Caught You Reading

JULY 2000

THE NEXT TIME SOMEONE TALKS about the narrow interests of
kids today, how they attend only to the raucous cry of the computer calling across a stretch of cable to its mate the Internet, remember this week. Remember how the boys and girls of America
went gaga over a book, a real old-fashioned black-letters-on-
white-paper book, how they waited in line for it at the mall,
cradled it to their bony little chests and carried it into their bedrooms, slipped into its imaginary world with big eyes and open
minds as children have done almost since Gutenberg put the
pedal to the metal of the printing press.

There's nothing so wonderful in America that someone can't
create a kind of Calvary out of it, and so it is with the publication
of the fourth Harry Potter book. It is called *Harry Potter and the
Goblet of Fire*, but it could just as well have been called *Harry
Potter and the Lingerie Sale at Saks* for all the difference a title
would have made in its reception. Bookstores stayed open after
midnight on opening day to accommodate the publisher's em-

bargo; children dressed up like Harry and the rest of the gang at the Hogwarts School. And this was characterized as the triumph of hype, and the legerdemain of marketing. But hype and marketing go only so far when a twelve-year-old settles down on the sofa for the long haul with a book longer than *Crime and Punishment*. What remains is wonderfully retro: the beauty of reading for pleasure, and its enduring role in the life of the mind.

Yes, yes, of course you've heard that reading has gone out of fashion. It makes you wonder how the other three Harry Potter books have managed to sell more copies than there are people living in Greece and Hungary combined. It makes you wonder why Barnes and Noble stores spring up everywhere like mushrooms after a rainy spell. And how can it be that *A Tree Grows in Brooklyn*, a coming-of-age story set in 1912 and published in 1943, refuses to go out of print, that *Our Town* sold seventy thousand paperback copies last year? That's a whole lot of school plays.

The answer is that reports of the death of the book have been greatly exaggerated. It is indeed true that a recent study of a representative sample of Americans found that the number of people who read for more than thirty minutes a day had dropped from 51 to 45 percent. But a Gallup poll of Americans' favorite leisure activities also showed that more than one in four still put reading at or near the top of the list.

Some librarians over the age of seventy might insist that that can't compare to a half century ago, and although those are the wise human beings who first introduced us to the Betsy-Tacy books and *A Girl of the Limberlost*, they would be wrong. In 1952, to the question "Do you happen to be reading any books or novels at the present time?" only 18 percent of Americans surveyed by Gallup said yes. In 1963 fewer than half the Americans polled said they had read a book all the way through in the last year; in 1999 that number was 84 percent.

There have always been Americans who did not care to read. Years ago they had to bring in the hay and make house calls, and in their spare time they wanted to play bridge and shoot pool. Today they slave over a hot computer or say "Would you like to supersize that?" and in their spare time they want to talk online to strangers and watch Jennifer Aniston's hair grow on television. Parents increasingly worry that their children are not reading enough. The most curious of these are parents who have shelves full of stereo equipment and not a single book in the house, whose children have only seen them read *Car and Driver* while waiting at the Quik Lube.

The spectacular success of the Harry Potter books might help create a new generation of inveterate readers. At the very least it provides a soothing reminder that well-written stories with interesting characters manage to find an audience. You would not conclude this from the keening of critics who insist the book is dead, the book is polluted by commerce, the book has been hijacked by Grisham and King and those novels in which darkly handsome men pretend not to be interested in spirited green-eyed heroines until the last twenty pages, when they take them in their arms and all kinds of stuff happens.

This dark view certainly offers the satisfaction of confirming our worst fears about human nature, but it does not have the advantage of being entirely accurate. Last year the collection *The Best American Short Stories* sold just as well as *Dilbert Gives You the Business.* Jacques Barzun, perhaps this country's best-known humanities scholar, has a new book, *From Dawn to Decadence,* with the surefire buy-me subtitle *500 Years of Western Cultural Life.* This great doorstop of a history became a bestseller almost as soon as it was in stores. It is one of those "surprise" bestsellers you hear about so often, since if it's gospel that Americans don't read, it's got to be a surprise when they buy literary novels like *Cold Mountain* or *The God of Small Things* or serious non-fiction books like *Longitude* or *Midnight in the Garden of Good and Evil.* Luckily there are such surprises every publishing season.

There will be no surprise at all when the newest Harry Potter book follows its older siblings to the top of the bestseller lists and, as important, into the hands and hearts of millions of readers. This has no more or less to do with hype than the success of a movie called *Gone with the Wind* did when the grandparents of these children were children themselves. It has a lot to do with characters who jump from a book as though they were grasshoppers trapped between the pages. "This is very weird, but quite possibly true," says one of the kids in *Summer Reading Is Killing Me!,* the Time Warp Trio book. "What if story characters are real in some way?" In fifty years, today's children will not remember who survived *Survivor*—actually, in a few weeks none of us will remember who survived *Survivor*—but they will remember Harry. They will remember this week.

With a No. 2 Pencil, Delete

JUNE 2002

YOU CAN IMAGINE HOW HONORED I was to learn that my work was going to be mangled for the sake of standardized testing. I got the word just after a vigilant parent had discovered that statewide English tests in New York had included excerpts from literary writers edited so heavily and so nonsensically that the work had essentially lost all meaning. Isaac Bashevis Singer, Annie Dillard, even Chekhov—the pool of those singled out for red-penciling by bureaucrats was a distinguished one, and I found myself a little disappointed that I had not been turned into reading comp pablum.

But the State of Georgia was more accommodating. The folks at the Educational Testing Service, one of America's most powerful monopolies and the entity responsible for the SATs, were preparing something called the Georgia End-of-Course Tests and wanted to use an excerpt from a book I'd written called *How Reading Changed My Life*.

In the sentence that read "The Sumerians first used the written word to make laundry lists, to keep track of cows and slaves and household goods," the words "and slaves" had been deleted.

And in the sentence "And soon publishers had the means, and the will, to publish anything—cookbooks, broadsides, newspapers, novels, poetry, pornography, picture books for children" someone had drawn a black line through the word "pornography" and written "EDIT!" in the margin.

I got off easy. In the Singer excerpt on the Regents exam, which was about growing up a Jew in prewar Poland, all references to Jews and Poles were excised. Annie Dillard's essay about being the only white child in a library in the black section of town became almost unintelligible after all references to race were obliterated. The New York State Education Department's overheated guidelines are written so broadly that only the words "the" and "but" seem safe. "Does the material require the parent, teacher or examinee to support a position that is contrary to their religious beliefs or teaching?" the guidelines ask. "Does the material assume that the examinee has experience with a certain type of family structure?" As Jeanne Heifetz, an opponent of the required Regents exams who uncovered the editing, wrote, "Almost no piece of writing emerges from this process unscathed." Nor could any except the most homogenized piece of pap about Cape Cod tide pools.

"The words 'slave' and 'pornography' deal with controversial issues that could cause an emotional reaction in some students that could distract them from the test and affect their performance," wrote the ETS supernumerary snipping at my sentences.

This was in a week when students likely heard of another suicide bomber in Israel, the gunpoint abduction of a teenager in Utah, and the arrest of a rap star for appearing on videotape having sex with underage girls. And they're going to be distracted by the words "slaves" and "pornography"?

That's the saddest thing here: not the betrayal of writers by bureaucrats, but the betrayal of kids by educators. Everyone complains that teenagers don't read enough good stuff; the lists of banned books in school libraries are thick with quality, with Steinbeck and Margaret Atwood. Everyone complains that students are not intellectually engaged; controversial issues are excised from classroom discussions and those staggeringly boring textbooks. Everyone complains that kids are not excited about school; the point of school increasingly seems to be mindless and incessant testing that doesn't even have the grace to be mildly interesting. By the standards of the Regents tests, *The Catcher in the Rye* is unacceptable. ("Does the material require a student to take a position that challenges parental authority?") So is *To Kill a Mockingbird* and *The Merchant of Venice*.

Here is the most shocking question among the New York State Education Department guidelines: "Does the material assume values not shared by all test takers?" There is no book worth reading, no poem worth writing, no essay worth analyzing, that assumes the same values for all. That sentence is the death of intellectual engagement.

The education officials in New York have now backed down from their cut-and-paste-without-permission position, faced with an angry mob of distinguished writers. But what do the kids learn from this? That the written word doesn't really matter much, that it can be weakened at will. That no one trusts a student to understand that variations in opinion and background are both objectively interesting and intellectually challenging. That some of the most powerful people involved in their education have reduced them to the lowest common denominator.

I like kids, have a brace of them around here, and I'm damned (EDIT!) if I'm going to abet some skewed adult vision of their febrile emotional state. Unlike those in New York, the people preparing tests for the State of Georgia at least had the common courtesy to ask permission to mess with my stuff. I declined. It's not that one or two words are particularly precious; I have hacked away at my own sentences to get them to fit tidily in this space. But not to make pablum for students who deserve something tastier.

Poetry Emotion

APRIL 1994

YUSEF KOMUNYAKAA WON THE PULITZER PRIZE this week, but he does not expect to become a household name, and not because his name itself, phonetically simple once parsed out bit by bit, looks at first glance so unpronounceable. Mr. Komunyakaa won the prize for poetry, and there is little premium in poetry in a world that thinks of Pound and Whitman as a weight and a sampler, not an Ezra, a Walt, a thing of beauty, a joy forever.

It's hard to figure out why this should be true, why poetry has been shunted onto a siding at a time, a place, so in need of brevity and truth. We still use the word as a synonym for a kind of lovely perfection, for an inspired figure skater, an accomplished ballet dancer. Many of the finest books children read when young are poetry: *The Cat in the Hat, Goodnight Moon,* the free verse of *Where the Wild Things Are.*

And then suddenly, just as their faces lose the soft curves of babyhood, the children harden into prose, and leave verse behind, or reject it entirely. Their summer reading lists rarely in-

259

clude poetry, only stories; *The Red Badge of Courage,* not Mr. Komunyakaa's spare and evocative poems about his hitch in Vietnam:

> *He danced with tall grass*
> *for a moment, like he was swaying*
> *with a woman. Our gun barrels*
> *glowed white-hot.*
> *When I got to him,*
> *a blue halo*
> *of flies had already claimed him.*

For some of those children who once were lulled to sleep by the rhythms of Seuss and Sendak, poetry comes now set to music: Nirvana and Arrested Development, Tori Amos and the Indigo Girls. Many readers are scared off young, put off by the belief that poetry is difficult and demanding. We complain that it doesn't sound like the way we talk, but if it sounds like the way we talk, we complain that it doesn't rhyme.

A poet who teaches in the schools tells of how one boy told him he couldn't, wouldn't write poetry. Then one day in class he heard Hayden Carruth's "Cows at Night" and cried, "I didn't know we were allowed to write poems about cows."

Or to write a poem about two women talking in the kitchen:

> *Crazy as a bessy bug.*
> *Jack wasn't cold*
> *In his grave before*
> *She done up & gave all*
> *The insurance money*
> *To some young pigeon*

Who never hit a lick
At work in his life.
He cleaned her out & left
With Donna Faye's girl.
Honey, hush. You don't
Say . . .

That's Mr. Komunyakaa, from the collection *Neon Vernacular,* which won the Pulitzer. His publisher originally printed 2,500 copies, which is fairly large for poetry but a joke to the folks who stock those racks at the airport. Few are the parents who leap up with soundless joy when a son or daughter announces, "Mom, Dad, I've decided to become a poet."

People who are knowledgeable about poetry sometimes discuss it in that knowing, rather hateful way in which oenophiles talk about wine: robust, delicate, muscular. This has nothing to do with how most of us experience it, the heart coming around the corner and unexpectedly running into the mind. Of all the words that have stuck to the ribs of my soul, poetry has been the most filling. Robert Frost, Robert Lowell, Elizabeth Bishop, Emily Dickinson, the divine W. B. Yeats. "April is the cruellest month." "O World, I cannot hold thee close enough!" "After the first death, there is no other." "A terrible beauty is born."

Poems are now appearing on posters in subway trains; one commuter said of a Langston Hughes poem, "I can't express it, but I get it." Now rolling through the soot-black dark of the tunnels and the surprising sunshine where the subways suddenly shoot above ground: Marianne Moore, William Carlos Williams, Audre Lorde, May Swenson, Rita Dove, and Gwendolyn Brooks, who wrote that exquisite evocation of carpe diem, and perhaps of poetry, too:

Exhaust the little moment. Soon it dies.
And be it gash or gold it will not come
Again in this identical disguise.

Says Mr. Komunyakaa, who teaches, "I never really approached it from the perspective of making a living. It was simply a need." Maybe it's a need for us all and we just forget it, as we move past bedtime-story rhythms and into a world without rhyme or reason.

In Memoriam:
One Real Pip

NOVEMBER 2001

THE AUCTIONEERS SOLD ALL of Maxine Smiley's things. The dry sink, the cherry chest of drawers, the round table with the lazy Susan that sat on the porch: All of them belong to someone else now. At least the house went to a family, people with children who are going to build something bigger up the hill, where the stream starts. The oil painting of the swamp with that strange yellow electrical storm light is now over the sideboard in our dining room. Someone else bid for me. I'll never enter that house again.

One woman of eighty-six who said matter-of-factly last Christmas, her husband and her sisters and all her friends gone, "I'm ready." Buried on September 10, on the last everyday morning of the rest of our lives. Terrorists marked the end of an era, but for me an era had already ended when I realized she would never again tell me she liked my hair better the other way. Why were the pews filled with middle-aged women, their faces crumpled and wet as the tissues in their fists? She seemed as good a candidate for immortality as anyone we'd ever known, with that strong character, that unflinching eye, those uncompromising opinions. You want role models? Oh, we had one.

"She was a pip," someone said after they'd seen the obituary in the local paper. That's code. It means direct, difficult, not to be trifled with: It's used mainly for women, in the same way that prickly is. When we bought the house next door our daughter and Mrs. Smiley became two pips in a pod We cut a hole in the hedge so the little girl could visit the old woman. "If I was mad at my mom and dad, I would go to her," Maria once wrote in an essay entitled "My Best Friend." Both of them were outspoken and stubborn. "It's time for you to go home now," Mrs. Smiley would say if Maria was becoming tiresome, and suddenly I would see a small figure flouncing across the lawn, skirts and curls in high dudgeon. "Mrs. Smiley is crabby!" she would growl, and bang the door.

In all the years I knew her I never told her I loved her, and I rarely called her by her first name. I suspect that was fine by her. I think she believed that all the fashionable mewling about feelings and all the casual informality were a cheap and easy substitute for something more difficult and more dignified. She did not pour out her heart, even over her habitual gin martini. She would have considered this tiresome, although her life story was not. She left a small town to go to Kansas City and become a nurse, then worked as one of the first flight attendants for TWA, went into the army during World War II, and spent several years of her middle age living on a sailboat. Amid all of this she fell in love with a married man, and later she married him herself. She was not ashamed of this but neither was she casual about it. In his eulogy her nephew said, "During the years before her marriage was approved by Church authorities, she played strictly by the rules, attending Mass every Sunday but never receiving Communion."

We shared recipes, not secrets or confidences. She was a woman who would eat alone on a television tray and have grilled salmon with a caper cream sauce and a Greek salad, and who would say, as we left a restaurant, "We could have done better at home." She refused to give up cigarettes and if you didn't like it, you didn't have to come around. She read omnivorously and self-diagnosed, mostly correctly, sometimes driving the doctors mad. If you complained about the development, the covey of ersatz colonials that had grown up around her barn, she would shrug. "People have to live somewhere," she said.

She was a character; that's code, too. It sometimes seems that in the name of psychological health or peaceful coexistence the people of this country have eliminated all the sharp elbows and hard edges from their personalities. Plain-vanilla politicians, leaders who seem less like Teddy Roosevelt than Ken dolls. From time to time someone bewails the lackluster characters moving like sleepwalkers through modern novels. But perhaps writers are only reflecting what they see around them, people who set their barometers to the comfort level of the greatest number of bystanders. Maybe the men and women of Dickens and Twain leap off the page because the men and women of their times did the same.

Maybe a nation as various as this one can only manage so much diversity at a time. When Mrs. Smiley was growing up in Beattie, Kansas, throwing such a tantrum once that her father dunked her headfirst into a rain barrel to cool her off, there wasn't much of what we mean by that term today. People who were not alike tended to live separately. The great diversity was in personality, the flagrant flirts, the solemn parsons, the wise women, the scolds.

Today, of course, even in some small towns there are Latinos and lesbian couples, interracial marriages, kids who can trace their lineage through Dublin, Moscow, and Milan. So colorful, except for character. The mute suburban housewives of *The Feminine Mystique* burst forth from their cable-knit prison to become surprisingly well behaved, knowing that not suffering fools gladly would be a real handicap in the world of work. Not suffering fools was one of Mrs. Smiley's hobbies. Two world wars, a depression, and all the hand grenades life throws at you: I guess the women of that now-evaporating generation figured they had nothing to lose by being their authentic selves.

Mrs. Smiley told me once that when she first started flying cross-country they would stop half a dozen times to refuel, and there were always passengers who got off and didn't get back on. The story was as much about the woman who stayed aloft as about the people who couldn't manage it. What was it they said about the old stars in *Sunset Boulevard*? They had faces then. And strong wills. And long memories. And guts. "Do NOT use flavored yogurt. PLAIN," says the handwritten blueberry muffin recipe she gave me. Yes ma'am. Whatever you say.

Imagining the Hansons

AS THE WIND BEGAN TO SHIFT northward and the ominous perfume of acrid smoke drifted down to the streets at the other end of the island, as the casualty lists grew longer and the stories of the missing less limned with hope, as the end of the world as we know it entered its postlude, it was the Hansons upon whom I fastened. No telling why, exactly, except perhaps for the way their names appeared on the flight list, with that single number:

Peter Hanson, Massachusetts
Susan Hanson, Massachusetts
Christine Hanson, 2, Massachusetts

I could see them clear as the lambent blue sky that seemed to mock the mangled streets of lower Manhattan. I could see them in my imagination, the part of my mind that veered away from the footage of the flames and the endlessly falling. Maybe Christine, two, had her own backpack to make her feel important, going on the airplane. Maybe her parents carried a car seat to keep her safe for takeoff and landing. It seems as though everyone had something that made them tremble: the airplane cell phone call from husband to wife saying he was going to take on the hijackers, the jaunty lament of the workers in the twin towers about the long climb down, the firefighters' helmets and boots found amid the rubble.

"It was the people jumping out of the building holding hands," a woman whispered at daybreak, walking her dog.

For me it was the Hansons. I don't know why. It wasn't even that I knew much about them, found out from news reports only that the three of them were going to visit family on the United flight from Boston to Los Angeles, the second plane to hit the World Trade Center. Instead I was struck by the idea of them, of what it feels like, to be a mother, a father, to travel with your husband, your wife, with your two-year-old daughter in the seat between you.

Despair was as thick in the air of the city as the smell of smoke. New Yorkers who often make eye contact only with the cement beneath their feet walked, half-dazed, glancing up at the sky that now seemed so dangerous. In the middle of the night, a plane flew low and loud, and we started from our beds, seeing the familiar urban constellation of white lights out the window, looking for the bombs bursting in air.

Hope lies in the bright line that divides us from the men who did this thing: We can imagine the Hansons. The terrorists thought they were destroying buildings, monuments to capitalism and American military strength. But what they were doing was blowing families to bits. They left behind, not so much a monumental mass of rubble, but tricycles, sweater drawers, love letters, flower beds, books, video cameras, unpaid bills, untidy kitchens, mothers, fathers, uncles, brothers, sons, daughters, friends, from Maine to California. And people have folded their hearts around all that messy detritus, so like their own, so that all the deaths have become a death in their family.

Anything can happen when human beings allow ideology to trump their humanity, when they elevate an idea above the lives of individuals. Anything can happen, and too often does. It becomes possible to bomb a black church and kill the four little girls inside. It becomes possible to execute a doctor who performs abortions, shoot him through the window of his own home while his children are nearby.

It becomes possible to drive a truck full of explosives into the side of the federal building in Oklahoma City and feel the ground buck beneath your feet, to turn a day care center into a conflagration and refer to the babies and toddlers killed as "collateral damage." Perhaps ideologues so divorced from empathy are incapable even of feeling for themselves. Hence Timothy McVeigh's dead eyes and stoic stare into the camera while he lay on a gurney in the death chamber. Hence the unthinkable willingness of the men who sent those planes like fiery torpedoes into public buildings to see themselves, as well as their passengers, as merely incidental cargo in the service of some heinous greater good.

As the ground smokes and the people seethe, it is tempting to feel something of what those men did, to see human beings as a faceless bloc, a wholesale locus for anger and revenge. In the line to give blood at the Red Cross, a man railed against the Palestinians because of television footage of men, women, and children dancing for joy at the thousands of American dead. But that footage shows other people passing behind the gaudy celebrants, people unremarked by the outraged and the vengeful, people who look away, who do not join in. The Islamic Cultural Center a block away from here has a police officer standing guard; in the middle of the night the roar of a man's voice shatters the street nearby, crying, "Every sand nigger must die!" Crazy, perhaps, but with a crater of tumbled steel where two of the world's most iconographic buildings once stood, the people muttering conspiracies to themselves on the street have overnight come to seem like seers.

Amazing, isn't it, the sort of plotting and scheming and careful planning that the blazing belief in violence to underscore demagoguery can produce? Amazing, isn't it, that without any plotting or planning at all, the notion that we are essentially alike leads human beings to rise up and, even stumbling about in the dark of horror, do what is necessary. Blood donations, bags of sandwiches, secondhand clothes, e-mail messages, casseroles, prayers, embraces. Evil requires careful machinations. Good does not. The end of the world came with both whimpers and bangs and all manner of sounds between. When it was done, what hung over it all, greater than the smoke or the shock, was the sense of what most people are really made of, the emotional alchemy that enables us, from time to time, to love our neighbors as ourselves. To see ourselves in them all: the executives, the waiters, the lawyers, the police officers, the father, the mother, the two-year-old girl off on an adventure, sitting safe between them, taking wing.

Everything Is
Under Control

SO I GO OVER TO THE SCHOOL to vote in the New York City primary and I'm in the booth looking at all the names and the levers and the sign at the top that says INFORMATION FOR VOTERS and it's déjà vu all over again. This is where I stood, this is what I did, just after eight on the morning of September 11. And suddenly I think that if I just stand still, don't flip the levers, don't leave the booth, that time will move backward, the spool rewind. I will come out into the bright sunlight instead of the steady drizzle, and downtown those thousands of people will go about an uneventful day, those hundreds of firefighters get called to a few uneventful fires, those passengers have an uneventful plane trip, those buildings stand until the glitter of the sun on their surfaces turns to the reflection of the stars on their night-black glass.

This is what is called a "control fantasy."

The country that once thought itself so different from the world, the city that once thought itself so different from the country, both are reduced to this: omnipotence dreams, endless what-ifs, sudden unaccountable outbursts of tears or temper, and guilt about anything approaching self-interest or pleasure. "Is it too soon to laugh?" asks an AOL online poll. "Is everyone all right in your household?" every business call begins.

Those Americans born after World War II are accustomed to a sense of control. They live in houses that need never grow too warm or too cold, with seasonal food available all year long, with televisions that get more channels than there are weeks in the year. They have molded their bodies and rebuilt their faces and lowered their cholesterol and raised their consciousness. Their children became the heirs to educational toys, soccer camps, community service, and universal college. When the facades fell to pieces on September 11, those children were uppermost in all our minds: nightmares, flashbacks, tremors, problems with eating, problems with sleeping, problems with trust. But the children are dealing with this better than the parents. "They usually resume their normal lives—and often do so more rapidly than we adults," said the article by a psychologist handed out by several Manhattan private schools. Perhaps it's because children never feel as if they have control of their lives, much less this generation of children, micromanaged into playdates and SAT tutoring sessions.

"Don't you feel that the world is a much more perilous place?" I asked my son.

"Mom, I always thought the world was a perilous place."

They've had a new expression over the last year, the kids: It's so random. Mom, that remark was so random. As always, the kids were ahead of the curve. Everything seems random now, the illusion of an ordered universe gone. Each airplane on the approach to Newark Airport seems sinister, each siren a harbinger of doom. People cry on the subway; someone passes a tissue. Visits to Disney World are way down, but Kleenex sales have surely skyrocketed. Citizens of the world at last, we can now imagine Beirut or Belfast. A friend who was moving from his native London to New York once told me that the difference between the resigned pragmatism of the British and the arrogant optimism of the Americans was the difference between getting bombed during the blitz and buying war bonds.

So much for arrogant optimism.

The left-wing information superhighway of fellow travelers sends its offerings to my cyberdoor. There is an antiwar petition with a list of signators, saying in part "Another senseless act of retaliation will not repair the damage done, nor bring back those who are lost." There is a message from an old friend urging the recipients to join the Arab American Anti-Discrimination Committee: "This is one way of letting other human beings from the most despised and terrified minority in the country know they're not alone." There's a great proposal from one man headed "Bomb them with butter" that suggests sending food to the Afghan people, adding "Seeing your family fully fed and the prospect of stability in terms of food and a future is a powerful deterrent to martyrdom." There's a feminist petition that says, sensibly, "We pledge to judge people by their acts, not the group into which they were born."

I agree with everything, and nothing at all. Part of the control fantasy is the notion that there must be some obvious way to respond to an act so enormous and transformative that it does not even have a name. (Tragedy? A play by Shakespeare. Terrorist act? Too clinical. Bombing? Incorrect and inadequate both.) But everyone knows that any obvious response is an oversimplification, that bombing Afghanistan to rubble is vainglorious, considering that much of it already is rubble, that the frustration with terrorism is that in terms of targets there is no *there* there. There's the temptation, too, to think that retaliation can mend what's broken here. After Tim McVeigh was executed, did the families of his victims feel more at peace? If Osama bin Laden and his followers are captured and killed, or if Afghan women and children die in their stead, will it quiet the ghosts of the dead downtown, carrying their briefcases and their take-out coffee?

There is a wonderful book for children by Lois Lowry called *The Giver* in which a stoic society assigns the role of feeling all the world's pain to a single individual. Sometimes it feels as if everyone in America has become that person. In almost every New York City store window, there is a flyer for a benefit, a relief effort, a fund. At the deli you can get one at the counter: "For relief supplies as needed: boots, gloves, dog food . . . To help police and their families affected by the WTC tragedy . . . Union fund to support the families of fallen firefighters." And as people pick them up you can almost hear them saying to themselves, yes, yes. I can do something. Boots, gloves, dog food. One of my friends is on the waiting list for a gas mask. Another is getting some putative anthrax vaccine. Things are under control. That's the lie we tell ourselves.

Honestly—You
Shouldn't Have

DECEMBER 2001

N.B. The following is the work of a recovering shopper.

ALL I WANT FOR CHRISTMAS is a box of my friend Ronnie's homemade peanut brittle, the sight of my children gathered around the fireside, and the assurance that the next plane on which I fly will not have a plastic tail that detaches upon takeoff.

I do not need an alpaca swing coat, a tourmaline brooch, a mixer with a dough hook, a CD player that works in the shower, another pair of boot-cut black pants, valences, shams (pun intended), lavender bath salts, vanilla candles, or a Kate Spade Gucci Prada Coach bag.

Like many Americans, I have everything I could want, and then some, and at this particular holiday season, in this particular year, the thought of shopping makes me feel like the little girl who eats the whole Whitman's Sampler (except for the chocolate-covered nuts) and washes it down with root beer. Uncontrollable consumerism has become a watchword of American culture despite regular and compelling calls for its end, but right now it feels more like an addiction than an indulgence. The United States has more malls than high schools; Americans spend more time shopping than reading.

Yet there's abroad in the land the notion that buying stuff at this moment in history constitutes a patriotic act, propping up the economy in the face of enemy attack. If maxing out your plastic at the Gap is what patriotism has come to, then all the stealth bombers in the world can't save us from ourselves. Said Adlai Stevenson half a century ago: "With the supermarket as our temple and the singing commercial as our litany, are we likely to fire the world with an irresistible vision of America's exalted purpose?" Put in the context of current events, how depressing was it to see Afghan citizens celebrating the end of tyranny by buying consumer electronics?

Some of the most insightful writing about the American character over the nation's history has been about neither freedom nor democracy, but about the crazed impulse to acquire things. A century ago, Thorstein Veblen wrote *The Theory of the Leisure Class*, coined the term "conspicuous consumption," and shocked his countrymen with the notion that the pride they took in their prosperity was the most primitive form of snobbery and self-doubt. He concluded that the buying habits of most Americans owed little to need and much to wanting "the esteem and envy of fellow men." Shopping even one hundred years ago was about insecurity, the need to exhibit superiority through gilt and cut glass, sterling spoons and spreading skirts.

Fast-forward to the present, and, despite what is described as a depressed retail climate, Veblen would feel utterly at home. There are still plenty of people buying cashmere sweaters and electronic gadgets, although the sweater drawer is full and the old VCR still blinks 12:00. But the urge for superiority today is more complex, Juliet Schor, a Harvard economist, writes in *The Overspent American.* When the term "keeping up with the Joneses" first came into vogue, what it meant was staying even with the most affluent family in the neighborhood, a yearning that was often within reach. According to Schor, television has meant keeping up with more remote and richer Joneses: the furniture on MTV Cribs or the endless home design shows, the clothes of Will and Grace and Katie and Matt. For most viewers, that's simply impossible, but they will go into debt trying.

There have been endless holiday pieces written about the bizarre chasm between the birth of a baby who couldn't even get a room, much less a suite with a phone in the bathroom, and the annual ritual of wild-eyed buying of items that, come December 26, seem beside the point. "Joy to the World" notwithstanding, Christmas shopping has become a joyless, even a hateful pursuit.

But Christmas this year could be rich, not only with lessons learned over two millennia, but those driven home in the last months. Not in my lifetime has this country had more reason to believe that "I'll be home for Christmas" is infinitely more important than "Santa Claus is coming to town." Yet some national leaders have exhorted Americans to shore up the economy and fly in the face of terrorism by saying, "I'll take it!" (Or, as one business type says to another in a recent *New Yorker* cartoon, "I figure if I don't have that third martini, then the terrorists win.") This brings to mind the work of John Kenneth Galbraith in the 1950s, which argued that the modern economy didn't flourish by satisfying the needs of consumers, but by creating the desire for products consumers didn't need at all.

The notion that we should show the terrorists who's boss by shoring up this shaky shantytown of automatic-pilot consumption is as ridiculous as bailing out the airline industry, a business that was poorly run long before September 11. When the shopping economy collapses, whether because of recession or national emergency, it's the system, not the shopper, that's to blame. Robert Reich, the former secretary of labor, has suggested alternatives to flag-waving retail therapy: a one-year cut in federal payroll taxes, or the promise on the part of leading corporations not to lay off workers for at least six months. And there are many charities hurting just as much as retailers and with a more essential product to sell: help for children who aren't eating regularly, old people who don't have heat, and adults who are homeless. The holidays should be a time to honor our best values, not a time to muffle them in layers of stuff.

Especially this year. You know that if those people whose family members died on September 11 could have them back for Christmas, the last thing on their minds would be a sweater or a tie. The truth is, those lost left their families and friends a bittersweet Christmas gift, an indelible lesson in what really matters. And they left that lesson to us, too. If we spend our Saturdays staggering under the weight of shopping bags, we're not honoring them, or doing the bad guys one better, no matter how much it may pump up the bottom line. We're showing that we didn't learn a thing, that at heart we are a marked-down nation.

Armed with Only a
Neutral Lipstick

MARCH 2002

GOOD NEWS, AMERICA: The airspace of this great nation is safe
from middle-aged women in business suits armed with twenty-
seven old crumpled Visa receipts and three identical tubes of
Bobbi Brown lipstick.

In the space of only eight hours I was pulled out of line, pat-
ted down, wanded, and, not to be coy, generally felt up at two
major airports. Twice, actually, at Chicago's O'Hare alone, once
at the end of a security checkpoint line reminiscent of what our
ancestors experienced at Ellis Island and again at the gate.

"Do you mind if I feel your back?" said a woman in uniform.
"If I mind, does that mean I spend the day with an FBI agent in
a room painted the color of overcooked broccoli?" I replied.

Actually, I just shook my head. And as I stood with my arms
outstretched having my ankles squeezed and my shoulders pat-
ted, as the other passengers filed by with that I-wonder-what-
exactly-are-her-ties-to-Osama-bin-Laden look, I did a little math
in my head.

Number of September 11 terrorists who were female: 0.

Number of recent incidents in which women rushed cockpits, lit shoe bombs, or otherwise ran amok on planes: 0.

Number of recent airplane hijackings by women: 0.

Finally seated, trying to cut chicken with a plastic knife and a metal fork, I came to three conclusions:

Airlines have not yet figured out that you can do more damage with a fork than a butter knife.

Women are too busy making pediatricians' appointments, having mammograms, and blowing the whistle on suspect accounting practices to hijack planes.

Airport security is a mess.

Sure, the administration announced last week that it is recruiting thirty thousand people to work as screeners. But if they're working with the same sort of topsy-turvy rules that dictated that I was a likely candidate to be given the twice-over, all that will be a waste of taxpayers' money. They're not only searching my purse, they're picking my pocket.

"The computer picked you," one of the screeners at O'Hare confided. Apparently that might have been because I didn't check a bag, or because I changed my return flight at the last moment. Of course, this is a description of virtually every frequent business flyer in the country. We don't check bags because the airlines lose them; we change our return flights because the airline canceled the one we were originally scheduled to take.

But the best guess is that I was snagged randomly because the airlines are terrified of being accused of profiling, and paying special attention to people who are not at the faintest risk as a security threat is one way to defuse that charge. There was a great uproar about profiling several years ago when a commission on airline safety recommended that automated passenger profiles be developed. Civil libertarians jumped all over this proposal, saying that law-abiding Arab-American men were likely to be unfairly singled out.

In the aftermath of the September terrorist attacks, conservatives jumped on those civil libertarians, saying that it was worth inconveniencing, perhaps even humiliating Arab Americans for the greater good, and that selective screening might have helped avert the attacks. Those arguments collapsed amid reports that nine of the September 11 hijackers were indeed specially screened, which obviously had no effect on the security of the country.

Somewhere there must be a middle ground between random screening, which is useless, and screening that targets only ethnicity and race, which is offensive. It is a middle ground that recognizes the difference between profiling based on bias, like the kind that leads to all twenty-one-year-old black men in Camaros being pulled over on Route 80 in New Jersey, and profiling based on information, as when members of a dangerous organization based in the Middle East are in the business of air hijackings. Of course there have to be other considerations. Age is one, since the average known age of the hijackers was under thirty. Gender is clearly key, despite the sudden spate of three suicide bombings in Israel by women. Citizenship, flying patterns, method of payment: The glory of software is its ability to take stacks of facts and pull out statistical probabilities.

Instead kids and old people are being pulled out of line for special security scanning, as well as a former governor of South Dakota who was flagged in part because he had his congressional Medal of Honor in his pocket, and a member of Congress who was asked to drop his pants when his artificial hip set off the metal detectors. My objection isn't that having strangers feel you up is creepy, although it is, or that it makes you angry when it happens three times in one day, although it does. It's that it's a waste of scarce resources. Who knows who could be sliding by while security personnel are checking my lipstick for plasticine?

One ubiquitous suggestion is that there should be a special identification card for those who are willing to undergo, perhaps even to pay for, the background screening that many civil libertarians decry. Another is that a risk-benefit consensus be built by telling Americans more about how profiles are developed and how well they serve their purpose. Right now, though, it's hard to shake loose any real inside information on how the process works. So I can only make some modest suggestions for airline passengers hoping to limit physical contact to their masseuse and their spouse.

Leave the congressional Medal of Honor at home. Once it was a mark of valor. Now it's just sharp metal.

Don't wear socks with holes. They make you take off your shoes.

Lingerie manufacturers: Start making bras with plastic hardware. Apparently there is fear that some woman will whip out her underwire and use it as a weapon. Quite frankly, by the time I was done at the airport I was more than willing to try.

Weren't We All So Young Then?

DECEMBER 2001

NIGHTFALL IS AS DRAMATIC AS THE CITY itself in the days surrounding the winter solstice. The gray comes down fast, pearl to iron to charcoal in a matter of minutes, muting the hard edges of the buildings until in the end they seem to disappear, to be replaced by floating rectangles of lantern yellow and silvered white. In the space of an hour, the city turns from edge to glow, steel to light.

Because of this effect it is possible, at least when the moon is on the wane, to stand on Greenwich north of Canal and imagine that in the darkness to the south stand the twin towers of the Trade Center. It is just that someone has forgotten to put the lights on, leaving the two giants to brood invisible in the night.

In the daylight the illusion vanishes. At the familiar corner of Park Place and Greenwich, it is the utter blankness, the blue sky and skudding clouds above acres of jagged flattened debris, that stun me as I stand for the first time amid the cops, the construction workers, and the tourists. "It sounds so stupid," I said to a police officer with his collar up against a stiff wind that carried grit and the smell of stale smoke. "But I just can't believe it's gone."

"It doesn't sound stupid," he said. "I say the same thing every time I'm here."

Twenty-five years ago my almost-husband and I lived in our first real apartment a mile away from those buildings, which were newly launched themselves. They were an unmistakable landmark for two neophyte runners: to aim for, to circle, to start north from again. They did not please the eye, but they boggled the mind, the arrogance of them, the confidence of their vertical reach, the symbol of a city that was sometimes graceless and always brash but never apologetic or unsure of itself.

That was what we wanted for ourselves. We were young then. "Weren't we young then?" one middle-aged acquaintance of mine asked a friend, but he was talking just the other day about that time so long ago, in August. On New Year's Eve in 1999, we all held our breath at the end-of-the-millennium parties throughout the city, waiting for the Y2K bug to bite. The phones stayed on, the planes still flew, the bank machines spit money, the towers remained alight. Relief. Reprieve. Revival. The deadline for the end of the world had passed without incident.

The date we all had written down for Armageddon, it would turn out, was the wrong date.

The twin towers were as much creatures of the baby boom as we, conceived in hubris in the halcyon days after World War II, developed during the optimistic sixties, launched in the seventies, bigger, better, more. The children whose progress mirrored the towers' own were forever young, a generation who had neither the tests of mettle of their predecessors, who knew about war shortages and breadlines, nor even the shadowed existence of their own children. The last generation of kids to ride bikes without helmets or pagers, we had childhoods before crime and sex before AIDS. We believed drugs could be recreational and drinking social, and the great formative trauma for those who evaded Vietnam was waiting in long lines for gas. What a charmed deluded life we led!

Gone. As gone as those monumental buildings. Tourists stand before the acres of nothing and take photographs. For someone who had a life intertwined with the towers, riding the train into its station, taking out-of-town guests to its roof for a drink, going to meetings in its offices, the gesture is bizarre. It is not that it is ghoulish, but that it is futile: There is nothing to photograph. There are signed T-shirts, used-up candles, bunches of flowers, crude crosses, Christmas wreaths laid at all the barricades. There is a small vainglorious handwritten sign for Whitehall Hardware among the maze of pedestrian detours, and an advertisement for condo lofts in a deserted building seared at its edges. There is a red crane, a black barrier, a series of handmade arrow signs at the entrance to what one policeman called "the main viewing area" that show Kabul in one direction and Staten Island in another. But mainly there is sky, so much sky, too much sky.

Gone: That is what death is. Disappeared. Erased. In its usual places the beloved object cannot be found. Rector Street. West Street. Park Place. The skyscrapers all around make the vast hole seem larger and more unnatural. Without the behemoths at their center they seem strangely denuded and vulnerable, or perhaps that is only projection on my part. The earth-colored spire of Trinity Church seems taller now without the Trade Center as its foil. The rounded headstones in the old churchyard behind its iron fence, worn and blurred by the passage of time, are instructive. Here lies a baby son, there a young wife. A daughter. A husband. Thomas. Sarah. Elizabeth. John. Once someone wept; once someone grieved. But it all happened so long ago that on some stones the dates of birth and death, the names and inscriptions, are almost indecipherable. A short walk from the mass burial ground where the twin towers fell, these long-ago losses have been muffled by the passage of centuries. But still they stare you in the face, bearing a message that is not eroded by the weather or the years: Forget me not.

People are changed forever by grief, and changed people change the way the world is, the kind of place it becomes. Getting on with life is not the same as getting over loss. The reports that Osama bin Laden may be buried beneath the rubble of a mountain cave have a certain symmetry. So many of his victims are beneath a mountain, too; if skyscrapers are the manmade topography of the modern world, this rubble was once our Everest. But if I found myself weeping as the clouds passed overhead untrammeled where they once gave way to infinite shafts of steel and glass, it was not for the buildings and not only for the dead buried beneath their ruins. It was for a time and a feeling as cocksure as the notion that two towers could rise high enough to nestle their heads in the clouds. It was for all of us who were so young once, in August, and will never feel that young again.

Look at What They've Done

JUNE 2002

THE SITE IS AS TIDY AND ANONYMOUS now as a hospital room after the patient has left, or died. The slabs of pale concrete look like the beginning of something, not its end, as though at any moment workers, whistling, carrying lunch, will arrive to begin to raise the girders and frame the walls as workers have done in New York City for as long as anyone can remember.

It does not look like a mass grave. It does not look like a crime scene. It does not look like a historical site. It is all of those things.

It looks like a development opportunity. And that it should not be.

Now that the wreckage of the World Trade Center has been cleared away, those left behind face a lesser, different sort of danger, but a danger nonetheless. And that is that what really happened here, the carnage and the suffering and the blind hatred and the sheer destruction will be muted by an impulse so strong that it may well count as a national disease. It has many names: moving ahead, getting past it, closure, healing.

But healing is for wounds. Grief is for deaths.

New York City is built on commerce, the capital of capitalism. So it was inevitable that when the silence became whispers, the whispers murmurs, the murmurs discussion, some of the first public conversations about the site of the most devastating injury in the nation's history would concern real estate development. "A fantastic opportunity," one architect called it. How pernicious is America's chronic amnesia that less than a year since those buildings dropped, taking thousands with them in pain and terror, what it all comes down to is square footage?

One of the earliest proposals for the site was for the world's tallest building at one end and a memorial at the other dominated by statues of two women representing the muses History and Memory, one holding a tablet, the other a torch. It is impossible to believe that anyone who thinks this event should be commemorated with a skyscraper and classical statuary has any idea what happened to that place, or this country.

This has always been a nation willing to sell out its past for putative progress. A new country, a young country, it sees itself always as a tabula rasa, which is why archival photographs of its greatest city show charming and even inspired buildings where now stand great hulking misanthropic glass cubes.

More cubes rise every day. There is the need for office space. The twin towers provided an acre of it on every floor.

But let them rise elsewhere. There is a great emptiness at the center of lower Manhattan now, sixteen acres of breathtaking ground-level flatness at the center of predictable vertical thrust. And that emptiness speaks as powerfully as anything can of the emptiness that it represents: not just the end of two buildings but of thousands of lives and a sense of indomitability whose loss is measured in eyes cast up on the city streets whenever a plane flies low.

It was a moment like no other in the country's history. It should be commemorated like no other. It should reflect what viewers see in *In Memoriam*, the stark and unflinching Memorial Day documentary that presents September 11, 2001, in all its awful magnitude. The occasional music to the HBO film is the heartbreaking Adagio for Strings by Samuel Barber, but the real soundtrack is the disembodied voices of people repeating these words: Oh my God. Oh my God.

Sometimes profanity becomes a prayer.

Once before in our recent past, history stood mutely waiting for the great right thing. Twenty years ago, anonymous entry 1026 won the design competition for a memorial to the most corrosive conflict in American history, the Vietnam War. An undergraduate at Yale, a twenty-one-year-old Chinese American woman named Maya Lin, had created in her mind's eye two walls of black polished granite in the shape of a broad V, inscribed with the names of the more than fifty thousand Americans who had died.

The design immediately came under virulent attack from veterans' groups and from conservative politicians. They wanted columns, flagpoles, a tablet, a torch, something redolent of that American sense that everything, eventually, can be transmuted into triumph. They could not see that Maya Lin's design was something different, something almost mystical, the visual evocation of all the things the war really represented, sorrow and pain and memory.

It is now the most visited memorial in Washington.

Perhaps another, smaller moment in history also suggests what the Trade Center site demands. It is the moment on *Air*

Force One, leaving Dallas, when Jacqueline Kennedy wiped her husband's blood from her face. "I should have left it there," she said later, "let them see what they've done."

The tragic cavern in lower Manhattan is not a design or a development problem but a test of the spiritual and emotional depth of an entire nation. The demands of democracy should not be confused with those of capitalism. To honor a tragedy of this magnitude requires a response of comparable magnitude. Maybe Maya Lin could suggest how best that could be done. But maybe, looking at the flattened plain where once so many worked and where so many died, the answer is to honor the emptiness by leaving it as a mute memorial. Are we a people so pinched of heart that we would trade memory for real estate? If so, the terrorists really have won.

One Day, Now
Broken in Two

SEPTEMBER 2002

SEPTEMBER 11 IS MY ELDEST CHILD'S BIRTHDAY. When he drove cross-country this spring and got pulled over for pushing the pedal on a couple of stretches of monotonous highway, two cops in two different states said more or less the same thing as they looked down at his license: "Aw, man, you were really born on 9/11?" Maybe it was coincidence, but in both cases he got a warning instead of a ticket.

Who are we now? A people who manage to get by with the help of the everyday, the ordinary, the mundane, the old familiar life muting the terror of the new reality. The day approaching will always be bifurcated for me: part September 11, the anniversary of one of the happiest days of my life, and part 9/11, the day America's mind reeled, its spine stiffened, and its heart broke.

That is how the country is now, split in two. The American people used their own simple routines to muffle the horror they felt looking at that indelible loop of tape—the plane, the flames, the plane, the fire, the falling bodies, the falling buildings. Amid the fear and the shock there were babies to be fed, dogs to be walked, jobs to be done. After the first months almost no one bought gas masks anymore; fewer people than expected in New York City asked for the counseling that had been provided as part of the official response. Slowly the planes filled up again. A kind of self-hypnosis prevailed, and these were the words used to induce the happy trance: Life goes on.

Who are we now? We are better people than we were before. That's what the optimists say, soothed by the vision of those standing in line to give blood and money and time at the outset, vowing to stop and smell the flowers as the weeks ticked by. We are people living in a world of cruelty and savagery. So say the pessimists. The realists insist that both are right, and, as always, they are correct.

We are people whose powers of imagination have been challenged by the revelations of the careful planning, the hidden leaders, the machinations from within a country of rubble and caves and desperate want, the willingness to slam headlong into one great technological achievement while piloting another as a way of despising modernity. Why do they hate us? some asked afterward, and many Americans were outraged at the question, confusing the search for motivation with mitigation. But quietly, as routine returned, a new routine based on a new bedrock of loss of innocence and loss of life, a new question crept almost undetected into the national psyche: Did we hate ourselves? Had we become a people who confused prosperity with probity, whose culture had become personified by oversized sneakers and KFC? Our own individual transformations made each of us wonder what our legacy would be if we left the world on a sunny September day with a to-do list floating down eighty stories to the street below.

So we looked at our lives a little harder, called our friends a little more often, hugged our kids a little tighter. And then we complained about the long lines at the airports. Time passed. The blade dulled. The edges softened. Except, of course, for those who lived through birthdays, anniversaries, holidays, without someone lost in the cloud of silvery dust, those families the living embodiment of what the whole nation had first felt and then learned not to feel.

We are people of two minds now, the one that looks forward and the one that unwillingly and unexpectedly flashes back. Flying over lower Manhattan, the passengers reflexively lean toward the skyline below, looking for ghost buildings. "Is everything back to normal?" someone asked me in another country not long ago, and I said yes. And no. The closest I could come to describing what I felt was to describe a bowl I had broken in two and beautifully mended. It holds everything it once did; the crack is scarcely visible. But I always know it's there. My eye worries it without even meaning to.

On September 10 of last year, my daughter and I went to the funeral of a neighbor we both loved greatly. We rushed home so I could go to the hospital, where my closest friend had just had serious surgery. Someone else took the cat to the vet after we discovered that he was poisoned and was near death. That night, as my daughter got ready for bed I said to her, without the slightest hint of hyperbole, "Don't worry, honey. We'll never again have a day as bad as this one."

Who are we now? We are people who know that we never understood what "bad day" meant until that morning that cracked our world cleanly in two, that day that made two days, September 11 and 9/11. The monstrous and the mundane. "Tell me how do you live brokenhearted?" Bruce Springsteen sings on his new album about the aftermath. September 11 is my boy's birthday. 9/11 is something else. That is the way we have to live, or we cannot really go on living at all.

We Are Here
for Andrea

SEPTEMBER 2003

A MOTLEY COLLECTION OF ITEMS has wound up on the bulletin board in the last year. There was a list of phone numbers for one kid's college, and now there is a list of phone numbers for another's. There are slips of paper with quotes from Margaret Mead and Hugo Black. There is the requisite fortune-cookie fortune: YOUR WORDS WILL HAVE A HYPNOTIC EFFECT ON OTHERS. There's a picture of the three kids together at Christmas and a postcard of a bulldog and an invitation to a book party I already attended and the instructions to the automatic outdoor light on the terrace and some business cards of people I will probably never call.

And then there's Andrea Haberman. When I was a kid, the nuns used to give us holy cards for special accomplishments, Saint Therese with her beauty-queen bunch of roses, Saint Andrew with his X-shaped cross. Andrea Haberman is my holy card now. Her face stares out into my office every day, a small laminated photograph that looks as if it was taken in a park, with sunshine gilding one edge of her long hair. She's smiling a little fixedly, the way most of us do in pictures unless we're taken by surprise. Above her face are the numbers 9-11-2001. Her father gave me two of these last year on the first anniversary of her death. One is in my wallet and one is on the bulletin board. I add things to the board all the time, but I never cover Andrea's face.

I don't really know much about her except what her father told me on very short acquaintance. She was twenty-five, working at the Chicago office of Carr Futures, came to New York on her first business trip and was on the ninety-second floor of the north tower when it was hit. She was from Wisconsin. She was engaged.

But that's more than hundreds of people who tried to rescue her knew. That's more than thousands of people who tried to find her body knew. That's more than millions of people who wept for her and all the others knew.

The morning that Andrea Haberman died is enshrined now in public memory as the last innocent morning in American life, before this country's people knew how much they were hated in the world, knew that home turf was no advantage, knew that the most invincible symbols of greatness were so vulnerable that they could be laid low in less time than it takes to read a newspaper.

Everyone believed at the time that we would never forget that lesson. Sometimes it seems it has already been forgotten.

But there was a more important lesson of that day, and it is infinitely more important that it be remembered. That morning marked the triumph of our best selves: the impatient martyrs of the fire companies who hurried up the stairs, the grimy angels with blowtorches who cleared away the steel, the heavenly chorus of people whose hearts seemed to lift from their bodies to touch the suffering of others. People fell and people rose, and the last is the lesson.

On this second anniversary the president proclaimed September 11 Patriot Day. That isn't the point. This is not a story about America vanquishing its enemies; sadly, the contrary was the case. But it is about good wrestling with evil and refusing to cede the field. It is a story of the power of love and of memory, of a stranger who hands you a laminated photograph of his daughter and so hands you an opportunity, every day, to remember what truly matters just by looking up a little.

September 11 should be formally made a day of nationwide remembrance by Congress. But it should become a day unlike any other so recognized, not a holiday, but a holy day. Not an excuse for white sales or four-day weekends, but a day of national service in the spirit of the spirit that animated so many after this monumental tragedy. It could be a day on which millions of Americans give blood, or deliver canned goods to soup kitchens and food pantries, or bring new books to schools and libraries. It could be a day of service on which every American asks and answers the question that united so many on that first September 11: How can I help? It could be a day on which, each year, we resurrect our best selves and by living with purpose honor those who died.

There has been a lot of talk about moving on, now that two years have passed. That talk is tragic. It is time for the United States to grow up and learn that history is not served by turning your back on it, that there are some things that cannot be smoothed over. Nor need they be. It is not an either/or, memory and solace.

Andrea Haberman is wearing her engagement ring in the picture, I think. Maybe she had just gotten it, was still in that stage when you unconsciously gesture with your left hand because you feel as if it's glowing. She is alive in the picture. WE ARE HERE FOR ANDREA HABERMAN, it says at the top of my holy card, and it is like a haiku of a prayer. That's it, you see, that's what was so extraordinary about that day. You didn't know her, and neither did I, but in our own way we were there that day, with a compassionate yearning. If emotion could transmit electrical impulses, all of us together would have lit up the United States like a great lighthouse for the rest of the world, like everything we wish we could be. We must preserve that somehow. We cannot let it fade.

Every Day, Angels

DECEMBER 1994

IN OCTOBER 1992 AN OBITUARY with this headline ran in *The New York Times:* HAROLD BROWN SR., 61, INVESTMENT EXECUTIVE. That description was right, as far as it went, but it did not capture the essence of Mr. Brown's life. If it had, it would have read: HAROLD BROWN SR., 61, DID GOOD.

For a long time I've been meaning to write this particular column, and it's somehow fitting that it turns out to be my last. For more than twenty years I've been a reporter, a job that people say is sure to make you cynical and has somehow only left me more idealistic. For the last five I've been here, in this space, considering the great issues of the day.

But the great issues, at base, are the same as they were when John the Baptist said, "He that has two coats, let him give one to him that has none." The great issues are the same as they were when Charles Dickens created the ghost of Jacob Marley, misanthropic man of business. "Mankind was my business," the specter cried, the lesson learned too late. "The common welfare was my business."

That is the most important thing I have learned in the newspaper business, that our business is one another. Time after time, story after story, I have learned it from everyday angels. Mr. Brown, who saw the homeless on midtown subway grates and, instead of looking away, organized a small shelter in his parish church, was one. So was Arlene Carmen, who died earlier this year; she spent her nights in a van on Eighth Avenue, bringing coffee and cake and a place to consider the future to street prostitutes.

Like Ebenezer Scrooge, I've walked the streets, seen goodness in the dark places, and shed the frosty rime that's said to come with my profession. I've visited the Holy Apostles Soup Kitchen in Manhattan, where every day volunteers feed one thousand hungry people, and the York Street Project in Jersey City, home and school alike for women looking for a second chance. I've been to schools where teachers bring imagination and intellect to life, and hospitals where the nurses bring comfort and joy.

This morning I could visit Tavern on the Green, where the Robin Hood Foundation is having its annual breakfast. Founded by three anti-Marleys, Wall Street traders who cleaned up bigtime in the eighties and decided to invest in empathy, the foundation gives money to groups that shelter, feed, and fight for the city's poor. Leaders of those groups will speak of their work, and the who's who audience will, as always, be dazzled by the simple spectacle of unabashed humanity.

They do dazzle, the everyday angels, just as the angel did in the Christmas story, scaring the wits out of the shepherds. But the angel said "Fear not," and that's what I've learned from its contemporary counterparts—the rape counselors, the good cops, the nuns, the librarians. Life will be hard, politics will be mean, money will be scarce, bluster will be plentiful. Yet somehow good will be done.

I've been lucky to be in this business at a time that was infinitely interesting, when women were more welcome. I've been lucky to work at a newspaper that stands for the very best that newspapers can provide, lucky to have had a conversation in print with millions of familiar strangers. I've gone places I never would have gone, met people I never would have met.

The greatest of them are these: Ellen Baxter, Al Cohall, Steven McDonald, all the others—you know who you are. You stand in opposition to a spiritual isolationism that makes icicles of our insides and a hard little lump of coal of our hearts. KARMA IS A BOOMERANG, it says on the tip cup at a Village coffee bar. If we do not reach out, it is we who will be alone.

The great issues are the same as they were when fifteen-year-old Anne Frank, three weeks shy of discovery in her attic hideaway, less than a year from death in Bergen-Belsen, wrote in her shabby plaid diary: "In spite of everything I still believe that people are really good at heart."

Fear not; Anne was right. The heavenly hosts prove it every day, in Coney Island, in Washington Heights, in Flushing, with cots, with comfort, with boxes of tissues on their desks. I leave you with good tidings of great joy: Those who shun the prevailing winds of cynicism and anomie can truly fly.

At the Left Hand
of God

RECENTLY, A MAN WHO WAS ENRAGED BY MY COLUMN sent
an e-mail with an exultant sign-off line. He said that in closing
he was not only going to mention God, he was going to capitalize
the G because he knew it made liberals like me crazy.

Five of the seven sacraments (they won't give me holy orders,
and I'm not ready for last rites), ten years with the nuns, a church
wedding, three baptized babies, endless fights as they grew over
why they had to go to mass on Sunday and a fair amount of
prayer, and it's all wiped out in a single assumption about the
nexus between left-leaning politics and atheism. A widespread
assumption, too, and one that has come to color, even poison,
American political discourse. It was inevitable that the opposite
of the religious right would become the irreligious left. It just
doesn't happen to be accurate.

When did it first become gospel that only conservatives knew
God? It sure wasn't true forty years ago for a Roman Catholic kid
in a Catholic neighborhood, when the knock on John F. Kennedy

was that religion was likely to be too much a part of his politics and he'd be on the phone to the Holy See so often the pope would be a de facto cabinet member. Jimmy Carter's faith was as much a part of his persona as that Chiclets smile, and I'd like to meet the guy who could go head to head with Mario Cuomo on theology and not cry for mercy by the end of the exercise.

All that made perfect sense to me because I had long ago concluded that I had become a liberal largely through religion. Loving your neighbor as yourself, giving your cloak to the man who had none, blessed are the peacemakers: Taken together, all of it seemed a clarion call to social justice and the obligation of individuals and institutions to help those who needed help. Jesus was the first radical rabble-rouser I'd ever read about in school, and the best.

Yet the other night I listened to Bill O'Reilly speak of "secularists" on Fox News, and as I tried to parse out who those secularists might be, I discovered to my surprise that they would be me. From same-sex marriage to Mel Gibson's gory cinematic take on the Crucifixion, the new wedge issue is religiosity, not to be confused with faith. This was fomented by the widely ballyhooed "worship gap" of the 2000 presidential election. The poll results seemed decisive, even damning: If you went to church more than once a week, you were likely to support George W. Bush by a two-to-one margin. If you never went, you supported Al Gore in the same proportions. "Capital G" and "small g" voters: there was the divide, as clear—and perhaps along the same lines—as the one between heaven and hell.

The problem with that easy equation is that, like so much else in American politics, it worked the margins and muted the majority. Most voters neither go to church several times a week nor never set foot in one. American life takes place somewhere in the middle, and there the worship gap narrowed, if not downright disappeared. In fact, those who described themselves as church-goers "a few times a month" were more likely to support the liberal Democrat than the conservative Republican.

But once the dichotomy at the far margins was combined with the positions we liberals take on certain social issues, especially those related to the separation of church and state, what emerged was the knee-jerk assumption that those with left leanings were never people of faith. This was also complicated by the fact that many of us not only lack a simplistic way to talk about the subject but also resent even being asked to do it, to slap the contents of our soul down to establish the bona fides of our political positions. Those positions are the product of the ability humans have been given to reason, to interpret, and to understand, not some literal textual interpretation that makes dialogue or disagreement unnecessary or subversive. It is astonishing to me to hear preachers of various stripes take to the television pulpit and take positions based on their direct line to the Lord with none of the empathy, humility, or compassion Christ modeled in the New Testament. That is not my faith. I like this verse from Hebrews: "Faith is the substance of things hoped for, the evidence of things not seen."

Even saying that much makes me uneasy. Democratic politicians have had this problem, and the new conventional wisdom is that to overcome it they need to be doing a lot more public God talk. Forget that. Any time I hear a guy going on and on about how his road to the statehouse or the White House was paved with prayer (not to mention a good bit of soft money), I get the uncomfortable feeling he's doing what Mel Gibson has done with his movie: trading on God for personal gain. The modern version of thirty pieces of silver.

The connection between politics and religion for me lies in the motto of Cornelia Connelly, the Philadelphia wife and mother who founded the order of nuns by whom I was lucky enough to be educated: Actions, not words. Touch the sick, the poor, the children, the powerless, as Christ did, and never mind quoting Leviticus. For the record, I have never written the name of God without capitalizing the G. But that is the letter. What truly matters is the spirit.

ABOUT THE AUTHOR

ANNA QUINDLEN is the author of four novels—*Blessings, Black and Blue, One True Thing,* and *Object Lessons*—and six nonfiction books: *Being Perfect, Loud and Clear, A Short Guide to a Happy Life, Living Out Loud, Thinking Out Loud,* and *How Reading Changed My Life*. She has also written two children's books: *The Tree That Came to Stay* and *Happily Ever After*. Her *New York Times* column "Public & Private" won the Pulitzer Prize in 1992. Her column now appears every other week in *Newsweek*.